CPD for the Career Development Professional

A Handbook for Enhancing Practice

CPD for the Career Development Professional

A Handbook for Enhancing Practice

Siobhan Neary and
Claire Johnson

trotman t

CPD for the Career Development Professional: A Handbook for Enhancing Practice

This first edition published in 2016 by Trotman Publishing, a division of Crimson Publishing Ltd, 19–21c Charles Street, Bath BA1 1HX

Authors Siobhan Neary and Claire Johnson

British Library Cataloguing in Publication Data

A catalogue record for this book is available from the British Library

ISBN 978 184455 631 1

Please note that all websites given in this book are subject to change, so you may find that some of these sites in time may be renamed, merge with other sites or disappear.

Typeset by IDSUK(DataConnection) Ltd

Printed and bound in Malta by Gutenberg Press Ltd

Contents

Figures & Tables

About the authors

Siobhan Neary
Siobhan started her career in careers in 1990 as a schools' careers adviser, where she discovered she liked young people but not schools. She moved sideways and began working in colleges and with adults. As a result of Planned Happenstance, she began training community-based advisers in the Certificate in Adult Guidance, and became more involved in training and development of practitioners. Siobhan has worked in a variety of roles within the career development sector, including being a practitioner, lecturer, trainer and researcher and quality improvement consultant for the Guidance Council. She worked for a number of years as a freelance consultant before moving to the International Centre for Guidance Studies (iCeGS) at the University of Derby in 2005 to take up the role of Deputy Head (currently Acting Head), with responsibility for Continuous Professional Development (CPD). She has a Doctorate in Education, through which she examined the role of CPD in the development of professional identity.

Siobhan has previously been a director for the National Association for Educational Guidance for Adults (NAEGA), represents England on the Professional Standards Committee for the Career Development Institute (CDI) and is a Fellow of the National Institute for Career Education and Counselling (NICEC). Her research portfolio focuses on CPD and the professional identity of career practitioners. Her ambition is to produce the definitive work on the role of career discussions in the TV quiz show *Pointless*!

Claire Johnson
Claire began her professional career in 1986 as a careers officer in Bridlington. In the days before the internet or even a photocopier, the careers world was a very different place. Continuous Professional Development (CPD) meant training days and a file of memos to read or the occasional journal or magazine.

A light bulb moment happened when, as a newly appointed District Careers Manager, Claire undertook an NVQ Level 4 in Management and saw the benefits of work-based learning. This experience led to her becoming the manager for one of three national pilots for the NVQ 4 in Guidance and her future career in the development and delivery of qualifications for the sector.

Claire's employed career included co-writing the Qualification in Career Guidance (QCG); a secondment to the Department for Education and

Skills to pilot the QCG and work on the training for Connexions Personal Advisers; and a spell as Head of Professional Development for the Institute of Career Guidance.

Deciding that she needed a further challenge, in 2002 Claire became a freelance consultant, developing and delivering qualifications and project work for the Youth Justice Board, HM Prison Service and Connexions Direct. On behalf of Lifelong Learning UK, she wrote the Qualifications and Credit Framework (QCF) qualifications for the career development sector and was Chief Verifier for Oxford, Cambridge and RSA (OCR) examination boards and the qualifications in Employment Related Services.

The role of Career Development Institute (CDI) Professional Development Manager tempted Claire back into employment in 2014, and she is currently responsible for: the UK Register of Career Development Professionals; member engagement; supporting members and registrants to develop their skills and knowledge; the CPD Resources Area; management of the Awarding Body for the Qualification in Career Guidance (and Development) (QCG/D) and the development of the Career Development Sector Progression Pathway. She is also Secretary to the CDI Professional Standards Committee and a member of the Institute of Career Certification International (ICCI) Global Council.

Acknowledgements

We would like to thank a number of people for their support and encouragement with this book. They include Trotman Publishing, particularly Della Oliver, and our colleagues at the Career Development Institute and the International Centre for Guidance Studies who have supported and encouraged us with this venture. A number of professional colleagues have provided advice and guidance throughout the writing process; these have included, David Andrews, Anne Chant, Tristram Hooley, Nicki Moore and Erica Rowell and our case study contributors, Bev Ashby, Dave Cordle and Liz Reece. We are grateful to all the practitioners with whom we have worked over the years, as trainers we learn as much from you as you do from us. Finally, we are grateful to our families, who always provide unconditional support and cups of tea! Thank you Neil and David.

Permissions
The authors are grateful to the following authors/organisations for their kind permission to use their materials. Sue Beckingham: social multimedia tools; Career Development Institute (CDI): Career Development Sector Progression Pathway and list of National Occupational Standards: Career Development (NOS: CD); Alan Chapman/Businessballs: Conscious Competence Matrix table; the Chartered Institute of Personnel and Development (CIPD), London: Key Principles for CPD; Andy Friedman, Professional Associations Research Network (PARN): the role of professional bodies; the Institute of Career Certification International (ICCI): Core Competencies; the International Association for Education and Vocational Guidance (IAEVG): Ethical Standards; Network for Innovation in Career Guidance and Counselling in Europe (NICE) for providing us with up-to-date materials; Organisation for Economic Co-operation and Development (OECD): career guidance definition; the Quality Assurance Agency (QAA) for Higher Education 2016: Scottish Subject Benchmarks; Taylor & Francis Ltd: contextual analysis of the Conscious Competence Matrix.

Foreword

Career development work is now well over a century old. During this time, the services we provide have evolved in line with changes in society, technology and the needs of our clients. As a profession, we have developed and weathered frequent institutional reorganisations, changes of government, devolution and, in some instances, privatisation.

Over the years, the career development sector has grown and strengthened to become inclusive of a wider range of professionals working with a broader range of clients, including: those who work with young people in schools and colleges, with adults in further and higher education or with jobseekers; those who provide career development activities in workplaces; and those who offer a private service with individuals and organisations. The roles that practitioners fill have expanded, with many adding career development to existing roles and becoming increasingly more specialist as the needs of clients become more complex. This has led to the creation of an exceptionally diverse and dynamic occupational area.

All of these roles require practitioners to have a breadth and depth of skills and knowledge in order to meet client needs and provide services for individuals and organisations who demand enhanced quality, efficiency and cost-effective provision.

Acquiring these skills and knowledge, maintaining and developing them and, importantly, being able to advocate for the value of career development services, are key to the future progress of the profession. Yet, in straitened times, the resources, both time and money, are less the gift of the employer and increasingly the responsibility of the individual who wishes to enhance their professional practice.

Against this backdrop, this book contextualises Continuous Professional Development (CPD) for the career development sector. In a first for the sector, the authors – who are both experienced Registered Career Development Professionals – explore the value and need for CPD and its role as a cornerstone of professional practice. They offer practical insights on practitioner research and reflective practice before providing a wealth of information on the many ways in which CPD can be undertaken by both those who are employed or self-employed.

The career development profession has come a long way in the last hundred years. Whether you are training as a career development professional, are moving roles within the sector, have added career development to an existing professional role or have practised for many years, this very readable book will inspire you to enrich your professional practice and provide safe and effective career development services to everyone with whom you work for many years to come.

As Chief Executive of the UK-wide professional body for the career development sector, I am delighted to recommend this book and know that reading it will be CPD time well spent.

Jan Ellis
Chief Executive of the Career Development Institute
May 2016

1 | Introduction

In this chapter we introduce you to the book and the ways in which it can help you to enhance your professional practice through continuous professional development (CPD). Here we specifically focus on:

- the context for the book
- the focus and aim of the book
- the frameworks that can support CPD
- who should use the book and how.

The context

No occupation or career ever remains the same, and nor should it! The world we work in is dynamic, fluid and ever changing. As such, no matter what job is undertaken, practitioners are required to update, whether this is clinical practitioners updating their techniques, retail staff being updated with the latest point of sale technology or financial workers learning about new regulations and requirements. Everyone's role is continually changing, and those who work in the career development sector are no different.

Over the past 20 years or so those who work in a career development role across the UK have seen extensive and wide-ranging changes to their work context and the needs of the clients with whom they work. Careers work can, generally but not conclusively, be divided into two main territories: privately funded and publicly funded. By privately funded we mean services that are paid for either by an individual or a company and not from the public purse; this has more recently become a large and important part of the sector, particularly in the UK.

The majority of careers work – for example, work in schools, colleges, universities, public employment services, non-governmental organisations (NGOs), and the voluntary and community sectors – is generally funded through public finance, whether at European, national or local level. Many career development practitioners work for large providers, such as the National Careers Service in England, Skills Development Scotland (SDS), Careers Wales and Department for the Economy's Careers Service, Northern Ireland.

In recent years, particularly in England we have seen a rise in the number of self-employed career development practitioners, due to schools having the responsibility for providing careers services.

Many career development practitioners, having found themselves unemployed, have embarked on a new way of working, selling their services to the schools they previously worked for. This has resulted in some interesting new working models for the careers profession.

In schools in England there continues to be a growth in the range of individuals engaged in career and employability learning. This can include subject teachers who include information on careers within their subject; careers teachers who combine supporting the delivery of careers activities with their teaching commitments; careers leaders who coordinate careers, enterprise and work experience-related activities and the input from career advisers and senior leaders with overall responsibility for careers provision in the school.

There is also a growing private sector of career development professionals who may have come to the sector through other routes and focus predominantly on private work with individuals and businesses involving career coaching and talent management. This is an important and growing part of the sector which often straddles the public/private sector, offering a diverse range of services to support career development and management.

What this all means is that the careers sector is neither homogeneous nor stationary. Practitioners, regardless of where they work, will all have varying needs to ensure that their skills, knowledge and practice continue in parallel with the needs of clients in an ever-changing world.

The Career Development Institute (CDI) has recently developed a framework, the 'Career Development Sector Progression Pathway' (2015). This pathway (available at www.thecdi.net/Career-Development-Sector-Progression-Pathway) broadly represents the range of roles that exist within the three main constituent areas of practice, career education, career guidance/development and career coaching/talent management. This supports practitioners and those who may be interested in a career in careers to identify the qualifications and opportunities that exist for the roles. Underpinning all of these progression opportunities is the need to engage with and take ownership of your continuous professional development.

The focus and aim of the book

We have both worked in the career development sector for many years and have spent much of our time supporting practitioners to develop their practice. As such, we felt that, with the continued change that has impacted on careers practice, CPD is one of the most important components for developing a profession, for building confidence as a profession and for being able to articulate and justify ourselves as a profession.

Since 2013, in the UK, the Career Development Institute (CDI) has been working hard to support the careers profession and, particularly, to ensure standards across all constituencies and geographical locations. These approaches have resulted in:

- support for the range of new qualifications, which encourage progression within the sector, including the Qualifications and Credit Framework (QCF) Level 4 Diploma in Career Information and Advice, QCF Level 6 Diploma in Career Guidance and Development and the CDI Certificate in Careers Leadership
- a code of ethics, which supports and underpins professional practice
- a progression pathway, which documents the range of roles that exist within the career development sector, routes and the qualifications required to progress (see figure below)

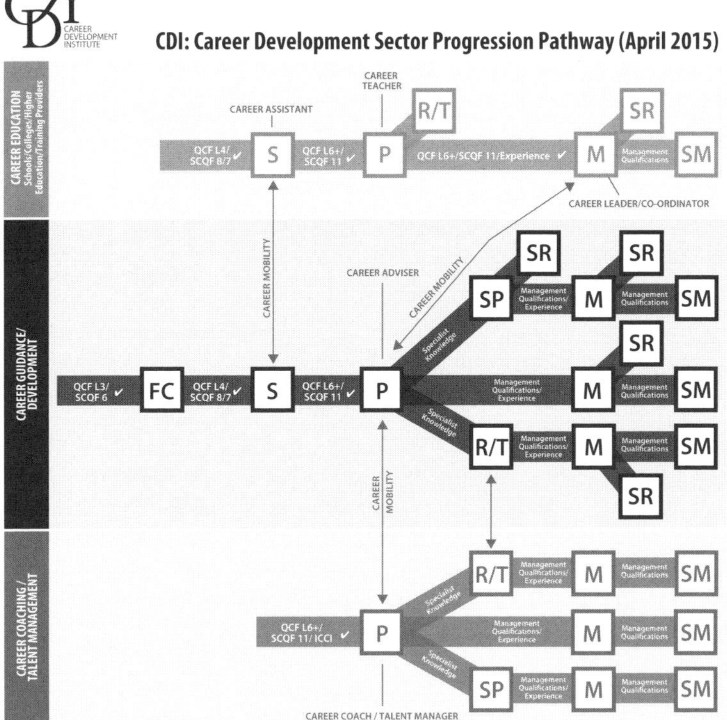

FC = First Contact / S = Support / P = Practitioner / SP = Specialist Practitioner / M = Manager / SR = Specialist Role (Lecturer/Consultancy/Inspectorate) / SM = Senior Manager / R/T = Research/Technical

Figure 1.1: CDI Career Development Sector Progression Pathway

(See inside front cover for a colour version of this figure.) Reproduced with kind permission from the CDI.

- the development of an updated set of National Occupational Standards: Career Development (NOS: CD), which support practitioners and employers in recruitment, initial training and CPD.

All of these activities contribute to supporting the profession to upskill and evolve. The purpose of this book is to focus on supporting those who work in the career development sector to enhance their practice through engagement in continuous professional development (CPD). It aims to support practitioners in all roles, at any stage of their career and in any career development context to reflect on what they do and to explore a range of practical CPD activities.

CPD is not just about attending a training session or reading the occasional labour market information (LMI) briefing; it is about ensuring that practice develops to both keep pace with developments and to drive practice forward. We will explore the purpose of CPD more fully in Chapter 2.

Throughout the book we use the term career development. This we feel suitably encompasses the various constituencies within the sector, such as careers education, career guidance/coaching and career coaching/consultancy/talent management, and is also inclusive of the types of activities which take place throughout the sector.

Frameworks for supporting CPD

Over recent years there have been a number of developments that focus on supporting careers practitioners. There is not room here to explore them all in detail but we do refer to them in Chapter 8. Here we just want to draw your attention to three which we think are of particular interest.

There is much talk about competence – what do we mean by competence? This term is often used to describe the skills, knowledge and behaviours required to be effective in a role. It is often the case that competence is considered within the context of initial learning and training, but there is often little mentioned about CPD post qualification. Our view is that competence is a continuous ability to perform effectively in a role; as such it is not a one-off thing. You may have been found competent when you did your initial training, but that could have been years ago, since when you may have changed job, moved professional context or started to work with a new client group. As Mulvey (2004) suggests below, initial training is only the start of the journey!

> *For those who do qualify and engage in autonomous professional practice, the realisation dawns that qualifying is not the point of arrival, but the point of departure.*

It is essential to be mindful when changing roles or responsibilities as to how competent you might feel within the new state you find yourself in.

Competence therefore needs to be kept in mind when investing in CPD; how will what you choose to do enhance your competence? We explore competence in more detail in Chapter 8. After all, you are either competent or not, and if not what do you need to do to become competent? The frameworks below can be useful in helping you to review your practice and consider your competence within the core activities. These frameworks have been developed recently and therefore represent the requirements in terms of current practice. These have been selected as they represent frameworks developed for the UK, Europe and internationally. It is useful to examine them all to assess their comparability. Below is a brief overview of each; there are a number of others that are referred to in Chapter 8.

National Occupational Standards: Career Development

The National Occupational Standards: Career Development (NOS: CD) were revised in 2014 to take account of how the work of the sector has evolved. The NOS: CD provide a framework that documents the key skills and knowledge that career development practitioners need to be able to demonstrate to be effective in their practice. The standards are multifunctional and can be used in a range of ways by employers and practitioners to support initial training and CPD. In the first instance, they provide a benchmark for practice. As such, practitioners can self-assess their professional practice in relation to each of the standards. Gaps in skill and knowledge can then be addressed and strategies put in place to address the gap or development need. This book will provide lots of examples of different types of CPD that can be used to do this.

Network for Innovation in Career Guidance and Counselling in Europe (NICE)

Another framework you may want to consider has been produced by NICE (Schiersmann et al., 2012). The NICE network is comprised of 45 higher education institutions representing most European countries. All offer programmes of study in vocational disciplines, career guidance and counselling. They have worked together to produce a handbook that outlines the key components that should be included in initial training. These components can also be used to explore opportunities for CPD; these are very broad ranging and provide a useful opportunity to reflect on existing practice and to identify opportunities for development.

The International Association for Educational and Vocational Guidance (IAEVG)

The IAEVG is an international body that supports the development of educational and vocational guidance and counselling. It has a large membership representing practitioners from across the world and seeks to advocate for high-quality educational and vocational guidance and counselling through working with policymakers and practitioners and promoting quality. As well as a competence framework, the IAEVG has also developed a set of ethical standards.

Who should use this book and how?

This book has been written with all career development practitioners in mind. That said, there are some who might find it of particular use at different times in their career; Table 1.1 below presents some examples of this.

Table 1.1: How practitioners can make use of this book

STAGE OF CAREER	HOW THE BOOK CAN HELP YOU
Newly qualified	• Provides opportunities to consider how you want to grow your career. • Provides types of experiences and activities that will contribute to your career development.
Experienced practitioner	• Provides examples of how you can look at your skills and knowledge and identify areas for enhancement. • Encourages you to share your experience with others.
Moving to a new part of the sector	• Provides examples of how you might build on your current experience and expertise. • Helps you to consider your networks and how you can build on them.
You are an employer/ manager/training manager	• Helps you to review the existing CPD offer. • Helps you to plan opportunities that may support your staff to take greater ownership of their professional development.
You are a trainer	• Provides useful resources and strategies linking to the National Occupational Standards. • Offers ideas to inform CPD programmes.
You are an initial training provider	• Supports you in educating your learners about the importance of CPD for ongoing professional development. • Provides resources and examples of how practitioners can build on their initial training to develop their practice.

Each chapter has been written as stand-alone, so you can choose to read the book chronologically or to dip in and out of the various chapters that may be of interest. It contains lots of ideas about CPD and how you can build an exciting package of CPD, take ownership of your professionalism and extend your expertise and the quality of career development activities you deliver.

Chapter 2 explores what CPD is and why it is important for our professional practice. It specifically focuses on why CPD is not just important for individual practitioners but also to all stakeholders. This chapter introduces the SOARS model of CPD, which provides a useful framework for planning and implementing your CPD in relation to self-awareness about what works for you and awareness of the wide range of CPD opportunities available. It also covers the importance of recording and reflecting on your CPD experience and its impact and the value of sharing your learning.

Chapter 3 focuses on professionalism in more detail; it considers what the career development profession is and what makes us professionals. This chapter explores the importance of theoretical knowledge and ethical practice. It addresses how we, as career development practitioners, demonstrate our professionalism through belonging to professional associations, the dissemination and sharing of research and effective practice and how we develop professional identity. It ends with an examination of how practitioners can promote themselves as professionals.

Chapter 4 focuses on one element of experiential learning, reflection. This is the most important activity of all CPD and development, as unless we are able to apply and review our learning it actually does not help us very much. This chapter introduces reflective practice and draws from key authors in this field, including Schön, Gibbs, Kolb and Bassot. All offer important ways to help us learn from what we do and to build our practice to support sustained development. This chapter offers lots of examples that will help you to integrate reflection into all your CPD activities and explore your comfort zone and how you might challenge yourself. It ends with supervision and how this can provide an important component of reflective CPD.

Chapter 5 addresses practitioner research as a way of both developing practice and contributing to extending the body of knowledge within the sector. As professionals we see problem solving as a key component of what we do, but how can we do this more consistently? Practitioner research is one way that career development practitioners can contribute to the development of practice. Here we examine how we might use other people's research to develop. This chapter provides a brief introduction to research methods and tools that will support you to identify areas for enquiry and plan, undertake, review and disseminate practitioner research. It will help you to start to build your knowledge of research practice and maximise the opportunities to share your learning with your colleagues.

Chapter 6 focuses on the needs of those practitioners who work for themselves. In recent years there has been an increase in the number of independent career practitioners working in all parts of the sector. This group has defined needs that are different from the needs of those who are employed by a company, where there will be a shared responsibility for CPD. For those who work on their own, often one of the scariest things is how you will keep yourself up to date and not be isolated. We know, as we have both worked for ourselves at different times. This chapter focuses on these needs through exploring self-sufficiency in CPD, developing professional networks, finding CPD to meet your needs, assessing your CPD needs and utilising the resources you have. We present a number of case studies of self-employed career development practitioners working in different parts of the sector, each of which provides examples of how practitioners have developed themselves and their practice.

Chapter 7 will help you to understand how the internet, and social media in particular, has influenced careers work. One of the biggest influences on career development work has been the internet; it has changed not only how we practise, but also the knowledge levels of our clients. The need for digital literacy is not just something that we need to talk to our clients about, it is something we as practitioners have to be more accomplished at. This chapter will introduce you to the importance of building a profile online and to the tools that can help you to build networks, expand your knowledge and to use social media as a central tool of CPD. It ends by exploring international opportunities for CPD and being a CPD tourist, building both your international network and your international profile.

Chapter 8 introduces a sample of standards and frameworks that can help you to structure your CPD formally and systematically. Practitioners across Europe and the globe are working to shared standards and frameworks. These frameworks offer a common approach to building practice. All of this helps to establish career development as a global profession with consistent and coherent approaches. This chapter will give you ideas on how to consider, focus and plan your individual CPD needs. It will provide you with a set of suggested activities that will help you focus on where you feel you would like to develop your skills, competencies and tools to enhance your professional practice.

Chapter 9 offers a plethora of examples of different CPD activities that you can engage with to support your own professional development. As with keeping fit, you do not need to have an expensive gym membership; what you do need is commitment and dedication. In this chapter we present an A to Z of CPD activities that will help you consider a wide range of opportunities that will both fit your needs and help you to develop your career. As career professionals we need to invest in ourselves, not just to provide the best service we can to our clients (which is, of course, important), but also to consider how we want our own careers to progress and develop. It is hard to talk to clients about future-proofing their careers if it is not something we have considered ourselves.

Chapter 10, the final chapter, provides ideas about how you can collectively engage in CPD, learn from others and maximise the strengths and knowledge of those you work with. It provides examples of how practitioners can use the learning from this book to plan and implement their own CPD. It also explores some opportunities and ideas for formal accreditation of learning.

Mulvey says that qualification is only the start of the journey, not the destination. We thoroughly subscribe to this. We want you to see this book as a way of taking responsibility for and guiding your own destination, wherever that may be. We hope you enjoy this book and have the opportunity to use the range of CPD activities that we cover. There are many practical activities and case studies throughout, which we think will help you to develop a deeper sense of your own needs, to assess how you might act upon them, apply the new learning, reflect and help you see how your practice has grown and been enhanced by your own investment in your career.

References

Bassot, B. (2013). *The Reflective Journal.* Basingstoke: Palgrave Macmillan.

Career Development Institute. (2014). *Code of Ethics.* Stourbridge: CDI. Available at: www.thecdi.net/Code-of-Ethics [Accessed 9 June, 2016].

Career Development Institute. (2015). *Career Development Progression Pathway.* Stourbridge: CDI. Available at: www.thecdi.net/Career-Development-Sector-Progression-Pathway [Accessed 9 June, 2016].

Career Development Institute. (2015). *National Occupational Standards: Career Development.* Stourbridge: CDI. Available at: www.thecdi.net/National-Occupational-Standards [Accessed 9 June, 2016].

Gibbs, G. (1988). *Learning by Doing.* Oxford: FEU.

International Association for Educational and Vocational Guidance (IAEVG). (2003). *International Career Competencies for*

Educational and Vocational Guidance Practitioners. Available at: http://iaevg.net/wp-content/uploads/Competencies-English1.pdf [Accessed 9 June, 2016].

Kolb, D.A. (1984). *Experiential Learning.* Englewood Cliffs, NJ: Prentice Hall.

Mulvey, R. (2004). Can I stop now? The role of continuing professional development in professional practice. In Reid, H. and Bimrose J. (Eds). *Constructing the future: Reflection on practice.* Stourbridge: Institute of Career Guidance.

Schiersmann, C., Ertelt, B-J., Katsarov, J., Mulvey, R., Reid, H., and Weber, P. (Eds). (2012). *NICE Handbook for the Academic Training of Career Guidance and Counselling Professionals.* Heidelberg: Heidelberg University. Available at: www.nice-network.eu/wp-content/uploads/2015/11/NICE_Handbook_full_version_online.pdf [Accessed 9 June, 2016].

Schön, D. (1987). *Educating the Reflective Practitioner.* San Francisco: Jossey Bass.

Useful resources

Remember this chapter provides a brief introduction and overview to the book. If you would like to explore some of the ideas we have talked about in more detail there are a number of resources below that can help you.

Hooley, T. and Barham, L. (2015). *Career Development Policy & Practice: The Tony Watts Reader.* Stafford: Highflyers.

Hooley, T., Watts, A.G., and Andrews, D. (2015). Teachers and Careers: The role of school teachers in delivering career and employability learning. Derby: International Centre for Guidance Studies (iCeGS), University of Derby. Available at: http://derby.openrepository.com/derby/handle/10545/346008 [Accessed 9 June, 2016].

Peck, D. (2004). *Careers Services: History, Policy and Practice in the United Kingdom.* London: RoutledgeFalmer.

Sultana, R. (2009). Competence and competence frameworks in career guidance: complex and contested concepts. *International Journal of Educational and Vocational Guidance,* (9), pp.15–30.

2 | Continuous professional development in the career development sector

Introduction

Continuous Professional Development (CPD) is a term that has become increasingly more prevalent in the career development sector in recent years as the demand for enhanced quality, effectiveness and cost effectiveness of the provision of services has grown from both clients and stakeholders. The sector and the roles within it have also evolved. You may have originally qualified as a Career Adviser and then diversified into career leadership in a school or into private practice. You may have trained as a teacher but now have, or wish to have, a role in either the delivery of careers or leading it within your institution. For whatever type of role at whichever level you perform it, and no matter the stage of your career, CPD is an important way of enhancing your skills and knowledge.

This chapter is about:

- what CPD is
- why we do CPD
- why CPD is important and to whom
- how to make CPD meaningful for yourself
- using Self-awareness, Opportunity awareness, Action, Recording, Reflecting and Sharing (SOARS) as a model for CPD.

What is Continuous Professional Development (CPD)?

One of the common definitions of Continuous Professional Development is that produced by Madden and Mitchell in 1993 through their study of the professions:

Continuous Professional Development is the maintenance and enhancement of the knowledge, expertise and competence of professionals throughout their careers according to a plan formulated with regard to the needs of the professional, the employer, the profession and society.

The Chartered Institute of Personnel and Development (CIPD) offers key principles for CPD, which are:

C - Continuing

- Members demonstrate their commitment to developing their competence through the virtuous circle of CPD.
- Development is continuous, in the sense that members actively seek to improve their knowledge, skills and performance.
- Regular investment of time and learning is seen as an essential part of professional life, not as an optional extra.

P - Professional

- Members show an active interest in the internal and external environment and in the continuous development and improvement of self and others at both organisational and individual levels.
- Outcomes should reflect the HR Profession Map.
- Learning objectives should be clear and serve individual and, ideally, client and organisational needs.

D - Development

- The starting point is a realistic assessment of what needs to be learned in order to meet the demands of the ever-changing professional and business worlds.
- Development is owned and managed by the individual, learning from all experiences, combined with reflection as a key activity.
- Working effectively and inclusively with colleagues, clients, stakeholders, customers, teams and individuals both within and outside of the organisation.

With the permission of the publisher, the Chartered Institute of Personnel and Development, London (www.cipd.co.uk).

For as long as there have been professions there has been continuous professional development. Anyone who has undertaken initial professional training, for example, doctor, lawyer, engineer, teacher or career adviser, career coach, career consultant, will have continued to develop their skills and knowledge throughout their professional career.

In recent years there has been a move towards the recording of the CPD undertaken and how this has impacted on and improved professional performance. For some professions this recording is part of professional registration and failure to do so can result in removal from a professional register.

The fact that CPD is often linked to professional registration, chartered status, abiding by a professional Code of Ethics and as a means of assuring professional credibility, has often meant that CPD is seen as being the sole preserve of the 'professional'. However, everything in this chapter can apply to any person working at any level and in any part of the sector who wishes to develop their practice and maintain their capability to remain effective.

The means by which people choose to meet their CPD needs can vary depending on who you ask. Some people use formal, accredited training undertaken post initial training. Others believe it to be the operational training provided by their employers to all staff. The latter can often be focused on developing the skills and knowledge required by law or to meet contractual obligations. Others see their day-to-day learning as contributing to their CPD. Neary (2016) identifies these three forms of CPD as:

- operational CPD – defined as mandated and directed by employers
- experiential CPD – defined as the development of tacit knowledge, skills and experiences with daily practice
- formal CPD – defined as accredited activities, conferences or input from external sources.

Neary identified that formal CPD was most valued, while operational CPD was valued least. Ideally, all of these forms of CPD have something to offer practitioners. Opportunities such as staff development or appraisal systems should be utilised by practitioners to focus on their individual needs as well as the needs of the employing organisation.

Some people, especially those who are self-employed, take a more personal, proactive approach based on self-analysis of their development needs and seek out varied means to address these, often using advances in technology to do so. Others look at how they perform their role and use this evaluation by self and others to reflect on what works, what needs improvement and then find ways to make these improvements. Luckily, there are only a few people who think that initial training means that they are fully competent and require no further development.

Doing nothing is not an option if you want to survive in the sector. Any methods of CPD are valid; which methods you employ is up to you as an individual based on your own identified needs, context, budget and motivation.

Why do we do CPD?

Initial training will equip you with a set of skills and knowledge to work in the career development sector, but nobody is the perfect practitioner at the end of this training nor could it be argued at the end of their career. The maintenance and improvements of skills and knowledge should be an ongoing process, determined by each individual professional based on their own needs. Allan and Moffett, writing in the *British Journal of Guidance & Counselling* in 2015, noted that:

> *There are perhaps two broad spectrums of competency in terms of professional behaviour. One is the concept that you need to be competent to start practising in a professional role and the other is that you need to remain competent to continue to do so.*
>
> *(Allan and Moffett, 2015: 4)*

They also state that many writers since the 1970s have referred to what has been called the 'competence cycle of learning'. The matrix below explains how this cycle works.

Table 2.1: Conscious Competence Matrix (Alan Chapman)

	competence	**incompetence**
	3 – conscious competence	**2 – conscious incompetence**
conscious	• the person achieves 'conscious competence' in a skill when they can perform it reliably at will • the person will need to concentrate and think in order to perform the skill • the person can perform the skill without assistance	• the person becomes aware of the existence and relevance of the skill • the person is therefore also aware of their deficiency in this area, ideally by attempting or trying to use the skill • the person realises that by improving their skill or ability in this area their effectiveness will improve

	• the person will not reliably perform the skill unless thinking about it – the skill is not yet 'second nature' or 'automatic' • the person should be able to demonstrate the skill to another, but is unlikely to be able to teach it well to another person • the person should ideally continue to practise the new skill, and if appropriate commit to becoming 'unconsciously competent' at the new skill • **practice** is the single most effective way to move from stage 3 to 4	• ideally the person has a measure of the extent of their deficiency in the relevant skill, and a measure of what level of skill is required for their own competence • the person ideally makes a commitment to learn and practise the new skill, and to move to the 'conscious competence' stage
	4 – unconscious competence	**1 – unconscious incompetence**
unconscious	• the skill becomes so practised that it enters the unconscious parts of the brain – it becomes 'second nature' • common examples are driving, sports activities, typing, manual dexterity tasks, listening and communicating • the person might now be able to teach others in the skill concerned, although after some time of being unconsciously competent the person might actually have difficulty in explaining exactly how they do it – the skill has become largely instinctual • this arguably gives rise to the need for long-standing unconscious competence to be checked periodically against new standards	• the person is not aware of the existence or relevance of the skill area • the person is not aware that they have a particular deficiency in the area concerned • the person must become conscious of their incompetence before development of the new skill or learning can begin • the aim of the trainee or learner and the trainer or teacher is to move the person into the 'conscious competence' stage, by demonstrating the skill or ability and the benefit that it will bring to the person's effectiveness

Allan and Moffett (2015) contextualise this for the career development sector:

> *When people are learning something new, they may pass through a first stage known as* ***unconscious incompetence****. Here a learner can be very excited about the prospect of learning but can often have very little idea of the complexities of the tasks in hand. They are unaware of the idea of ethical dilemmas and of the boundaries of their abilities.*
>
> *After some exposure to the discipline, the learner can become* ***consciously incompetent****. In this situation career guidance students and new practitioners recognise that they do not know how to do things and can often want to steer away from helping the client themselves and instead refer to colleagues, sometimes inappropriately. In this stage of the learning cycle, people might worry about facing ethical dilemmas, crossing boundaries in their competence, moving out of their comfort zone, and the potential to over- or indeed under-commit to their clients, all of which could result in anxiety about the consequences of what they are doing.*
>
> *The next stage in the cycle is being* ***consciously competent****. This is where the qualified or newly experienced career practitioner feels confident in their knowledge, is able to cope with a variety of complex cases and is trying to maintain their knowledge and skills by attending various courses and reading different articles and books. These practitioners take time to reflect on issues and can plan their career.*
>
> *The last stage is when the practitioner is* ***unconsciously competent****. Now, the practitioner incorporates their skills and knowledge almost without thinking; they will tend to reflect on something only when it goes wrong and, while they are happy to examine new approaches, may not recognise the necessity of continuing training to maintain existing skills.*

The need to undertake CPD is a key tenet of professional practice and a requirement of the professional codes of ethics for the sector. For example, the Career Development Institute's Code of Ethics says:

> *Members must maintain their professional competence, knowledge and skills through participation in continuous professional development informed by reflective practice and the National Occupational Standards: Career Development.*

The IAEVG Ethical Standards say that the responsibilities of individual practitioners include:

IAEVG members obtain the initial training and maintain a process of continuous learning in those areas of knowledge and skills required by the profession to be a qualified and competent practitioner of educational and vocational guidance. ...

IAEVG members continue to reflect in their practice both the humanistic principles that underlie ethical behaviour as well as attention to the changing social and political questions that have ethical implications for practice. These include such questions as who are my clients (students, workers, employers, society as a whole) and what are the ethical issues of importance in these relationships? How do different forms of intervention (individual counselling, group work, computer-assisted programs, and consultation with management on behalf of workers) differ in ethical concerns? How should educational and vocational guidance services ethically respond to the global tensions between economic and environmental issues in the working lives and workplaces of clients?

IAEVG members are responsible for monitoring and maintaining their professional competencies and obtaining training on a periodic basis to ensure that they are able to provide competent services to culturally diverse clients and to effectively use new theories and intervention techniques, computer applications, and assessment processes. IAEVG members strive to be current with innovations and trends in the contexts and content of educational and vocational guidance and counselling and do so with an acknowledgement that professional and personal experiences and growth go on throughout one's career.

The full IAEVG Ethical Standards can be accessed at: http://iaevg.net/iaevg.org/IAEVG/nave1ba.html?lang=2&menu=1&submenu=2.

None of us would want to visit a doctor who had done no CPD since qualifying, so why should a client trust a career development professional to advise them on their future career development if the practitioner had not updated their skills and knowledge?

Sadler-Smith, et al. (2000) found that the three main benefits of CPD for individuals were:

- updating (maintenance)
- competence (survival)
- enhanced (mobility).

CPD can help you to perform better in your role and boost your self-confidence, reduce your levels of stress, as well as giving you a competitive edge and potentially more earning potential.

Another compelling reason for undertaking CPD lies in the fact that the career development sector has changed significantly in recent years. Technological advances have changed the ways in which we work with clients and, in some cases, what were face-to-face interventions are now carried out by different media and sometimes with the client being in a different country. We explore this in more detail in Chapter 7.

Job security is no longer a certainty and a career is now more likely to involve more transitions. The skills, knowledge and experience that you have can offer you a more secure future if these are up to date and relevant for the evolving landscape. Progression pathways, such as the one developed by the Career Development Institute, can show you where your skills and knowledge can be used throughout the sector and where career mobility to different parts of the sector is possible.

For people who feel that the sector has become less professionalised, CPD offers the opportunity to reaffirm commitment to the profession, to remind themselves of and further develop the professional skills and knowledge at its heart and to provide effective career development services for clients who continue to value the profession.

Why is CPD important and to whom?

You

First and foremost, CPD should be important to you as a means of providing an effective and safe service for your clients, as well as the means to develop yourself professionally and personally. You should view CPD as a means of maintaining your professional health in the same way as regular visits to the doctor, optician or dentist can help maintain your physical well-being by diagnosing any problems and suggesting various means by which these can be addressed. To continue the analogy, undertaking CPD can also be seen as improving your professional fitness, which will help to future-proof yourself for the new demands in the sector and help you to secure employment or self-employment.

> *Everyone has inside of him a piece of good news. The good news is that you don't know how great you can be! How much you can love! What you can accomplish! And what your potential is!*
>
> *Anne Frank,* Diary of a Young Girl

Employers

Employers see CPD as important to the development of their staff and organisation. Staff whose skills and knowledge are out of date are a business liability, affecting client satisfaction and the meeting of targets; and this applies both to organisations where staff are funded by the state and to self-employed practitioners who rely on word of mouth for future business.

Employers also see CPD as a way of maintaining staff motivation and morale and the means to develop the organisation, unlock potential within it, help with succession planning and maintain a viable workforce. Being able to say that staff undertake CPD can also give employers a competitive edge, as this reassures stakeholders and clients of the quality of the career development services on offer.

In straitened times, when training budgets are low, employers often rely on staff to take responsibility for their own development, providing a minimum of in-house training but still valuing the need to have staff who are up to date with their skills and knowledge. Although this can be disheartening, especially for practitioners used to having staff development opportunities provided for them, it does offer the opportunity to really think what your own personal CPD needs are and to find more creative ways of addressing these, and so emphasise your true commitment to being a professional.

Professional bodies

Many professional bodies place a high value on CPD, making it a requirement of professional registration. The Professional Body Sector Review 2015, produced by the Professional Associations Research Network (PARN), states that 80% of professional bodies have a CPD scheme and that the scheme is compulsory (for at least some categories of members) for 53% of these, with participation monitored and sanctions in place for non-compliance.

Making CPD meaningful for yourself

As roles within the sector are becoming increasingly complex, lack of time is often cited as a reason for not undertaking any CPD. Some people working in the sector also perform a dual role. For example, those people who have a tutorial, teaching or leadership role in relation to careers in schools combine this alongside a main teaching role and face the challenge of maintaining their skills and knowledge for their teaching role as well as developing those for their careers role.

Cost and limited access are also given as reasons for not accessing CPD opportunities. People may also lack the time or willingness to reflect on the impact of any CPD that they do undertake. Some people are not natural reflectors. If you look back to your school days, were you a student who loved writing an essay following a school trip or the summer holiday and reflecting on what you had done and learned, or were you bored by this and wanting to move on to the next lesson?

In order to encourage yourself to undertake CPD it can be useful to develop some self-awareness about your approach to CPD. As someone practising in the sector, you will know that helping clients develop self-awareness is key to their being able to make effective career decisions, and that this can include considering how they learn best. Similarly, when planning your own CPD, as well as being aware of your professional strengths and areas for improvement, it is useful to consider your own learning style as well as which methods of learning and delivery media suit you.

The four learning styles identified by Honey and Mumford are:

- activist – people who learn by doing
- reflector – people who learn by observing and thinking about what happened
- theorist – people who like to understand the theory behind the actions
- pragmatist – people who need to be able to see how to put the learning into practice in the real world.

Although it can be argued that preferences affect the way in which a person learns, it is also useful if you look at developing strategies that help you adopt some of the other learning styles. For example, if you are a theorist, rather than simply reading theories it can also be useful to engage in training that looks at the theories and ways in which these can be used in practice with an opportunity to actually practise them as part of the session.

Also worth considering are factors such as:

- Do you learn well by yourself or is sharing ideas with others important to you?
- What motivates you?
- What ethical stance do you have?
- Why do you want to undertake this professional development?
- What time and budget is available for this?
- How will you know that you have succeeded?

Planning your CPD in relation to your own self-awareness of your professional needs and personal circumstances is more likely to be effective and you will feel more motivated to do it.

Your CPD needs and your preferred methods of learning can depend on your age and the stage of your career. Newly qualified practitioners may require reinforcement of the knowledge and skills learned as part of their initial training, whereas more experienced practitioners may want to specialise or learn how to pass their skills and knowledge on to others. Using technology for CPD may not appeal to all people, but sometimes using a medium of which you are uncertain can be a valuable learning experience in its own right and lead to future use. We often challenge clients about remaining in their comfort zone and sometimes it is good to challenge ourselves and 'feel the fear'.

How to plan your CPD

For all levels of roles, CPD has both time, cost and access implications and so it is important that you take steps to plan this carefully. By doing this you can then see how you have progressed from reflection on your practice through to the impact that your CPD has had. For professional-level staff it is the reflection on your CPD activities, how you have applied this to your practice and the impact this has on your clients which is required by professional bodies that demand CPD as part of professional registration, as well as the recording of the actual CPD undertaken.

CPD planning should not be viewed as a one-off event, but undertaken at least annually and reviewed at regular intervals depending on your own needs.

Many people working in the career development sector will be familiar with the work of Tony Watts and Bill Law (Law and Watts, 1977) and the DOTS model (Decision awareness; Opportunity awareness; Transitions and Self-awareness). Readers may also be familiar with the work of Kumar (2008) whose SOARing to Success model uses self-awareness as a starting point for Personal Development Planning (PDP) activities in higher education.

Our suggested model for planning CPD also uses the starting point of Self-awareness and then uses Opportunity awareness (of CPD opportunities), Action, Recording and Reflection and finally Sharing to complete the SOARS mnemonic. (See Figure 2.1 on the following page.)

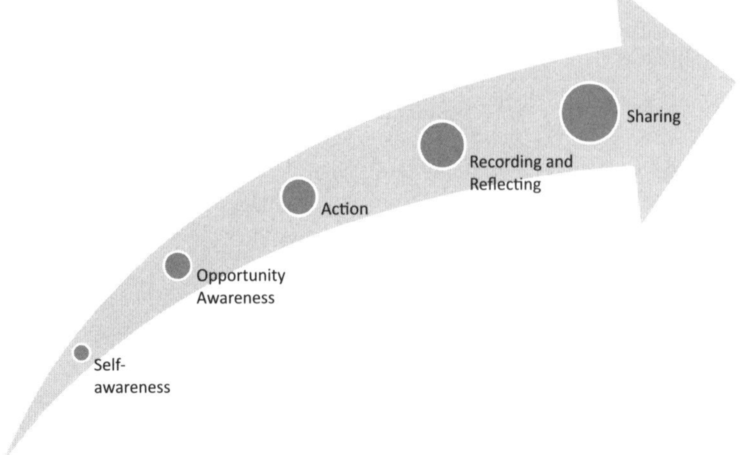

Stages	Steps
SELF-AWARENESS	1 Self-awareness
	2 Reflection on your professional practice and the context in which it is delivered
	3 Analysis to identify development needs
OPPORTUNITY AWARENESS	4 CPD Opportunity awareness and alertness
ACTION	5 Plan your CPD
	6 Undertake your CPD and put it into practice
RECORDING AND **R**EFLECTING	7 Record your CPD
	8 Reflect on how the CPD met your needs
	9 Reflect on the impact of the CPD undertaken on your work and any need for further development
SHARING	10 Share what you have learned with colleagues

Figure 2.1: CPD model SOARS

Self-awareness

As mentioned above, thinking about your preferred methods and styles of learning, what motivates you, how adaptable you are, why you want to undertake this professional development, your ethical stance, work context, what time and budget is available for CPD and how you will know that you have succeeded, is time well spent and can make your CPD experience more effective for you.

To determine what your professional practice should cover you can use standards and frameworks, such as the National Occupational Standards: Career Development (NOS: CD) or the IAEVG and NICE Frameworks, details of which appear in Chapter 8. For example, looking at the 17 NOS: CD will give you a complete overview of the functions performed in the sector and from these you can determine which ones are relevant for your own role. You can then look at the performance criteria and knowledge and understanding requirements and determine how well you meet each of them. From this, you can then determine any areas for development. Information on how to undertake reflective practice appears in Chapter 4.

Analysis to identify your development needs can use a variety of sources, for example, self-evaluation, reflection on your own practice, staff development reviews, observation of practice, appraisals, supervision, evaluations, feedback from clients and colleagues and assessments of your practice. These can all be used to show what you are doing well and can provide you with the opportunity to think through why this practice works and how you can develop it further, as well as helping you to identify any areas for improvement.

If you are wanting to progress in your career then looking at the CDI Career Development Sector Progression Pathway, which is based on the NOS: CD, will enable you to see which functions in your own role apply to other roles and which functions you may need to develop. Moving to a higher-level role or to a different branch of the sector may necessitate taking further qualifications. Details of which ones are appropriate are also provided in the pathway.

It is also useful to look at the national and local context in which you work and anticipate any changes that may impact on your role and future career direction. Information on the national contexts is available from professional bodies through email bulletins, government/assembly reports as well as any specific local information from your employer.

Being able to demonstrate to your employer how your CPD can also benefit the organisation by helping to meet business plan objectives, school targets or government/assembly contracts is also important and can help if you need to make a persuasive case for funding.

As the letter P in CPD can also stand for Personal, you may also want to look at your own personal development. Are there aspects that require development, such as time management, confidence about speaking in public, IT skills which if developed would help your performance at work?

Opportunity awareness and alertness for CPD

In the career development sector, we often talk to clients about opportunity awareness, usually in the context of what education, training and employment opportunities are available. Using labour market information (LMI) and being able to interpret it for clients forms a key part of the role of many practitioners.

Being aware of CPD opportunities and being able to interpret what is available for your own development is also a key skill for anyone working in this sector. Sometimes people will say that they do not have the time to research the different types of CPD on offer. To this end, being a member of a professional body – CDI, AGCAS (Association of Graduate Careers Advisory Services), CIPD, et al. – can be very helpful. Professional bodies such as these alert their members working at all levels in the sector about the training and conferences taking place, webinars and, where relevant, 'Communities of Interest'. They also have CPD resources areas, for example the CDI lists on their website, online, published and face-to-face CPD opportunities categorised by each of the 17 National Occupational Standards: Career Development (NOS: CD). There is also a section in which members can plan, record and reflect upon the CPD they have undertaken.

For those who perform a dual role in teaching or leading careers, the fact that you also have to keep your teaching skills and knowledge up to date presents you with an additional challenge. Careers teachers or leaders are often the only person performing that role in a school and so you do not have a department of colleagues with whom to share and develop your skills and knowledge.

Being alert to accessible ways of developing your careers knowledge and skills means that you may like to take advantage of virtual Communities of Interest, as offered by the CDI, or other networking opportunities so that you can meet people performing similar roles in other schools.

For those of you who wish to progress to higher roles in the same part of the sector or want to move between parts of the sector, then using either face-to-face or virtual networking opportunities can help you to seek advice from people who have already made this move and who can share information on what CPD they themselves undertook that helped them to progress.

Advances in technology now mean that more CPD opportunities can be accessed via the internet, which can be more effective in terms of cost and time. However, it is important to look at these and check that their content and method of delivery covers what you want to learn and that this way of learning suits you. Learning in isolation suits some people, but for others more learning can be derived by discussing their experiences with fellow practitioners. This is where social media – for example, LinkedIn Communities of Interest – can play an important role, as they enable virtual discussions to take place and can be particularly useful for follow-up discussions after individualised CPD.

Simply going to work can also be a CPD opportunity. In some respects every day can be seen as a training day. Being alert to naturally occurring opportunities to develop your learning is a skill worth developing. For example, a casual conversation with a colleague in which they share some useful information; a chat over lunch about an article you have read, what you learned and how you are now using this information, which then leads to further conversation on other ways of using this information, can be seen as CPD. If you also develop the habit of writing this down in a CPD record then the act of actually recording it can help to reinforce the learning.

Even when not at work some CPD can occur, for example, hearing on the radio about a new employer opening premises in your area or watching a relevant documentary can all add to your professional knowledge and keep you up to date.

An A to Z of different types of CPD appears in Chapter 9 and provides inspiration for many of the different types of CPD that can be used.

Having looked at your self-awareness of what you need from your CPD, what your actual professional development needs are and the range of CPD opportunities available, you will be in a position to take action and start planning your CPD. To help you structure this a CPD template can be found in Appendix 2.

Action (planning and undertaking CPD and putting it into practice)

When planning your CPD you should state:

- the reasons why you need this CPD
- a realistic timeline for achievement
- what the outcomes should be
- how you intend to put the learning into practice
- how you will measure success in terms of how well the CPD met your needs
- how you will measure the influence and impact it has had on your practice.

If your CPD involves learning a technical skill then scheduling in some time to practise it after the training is important for embedding the learning.

When planning any CPD activity you need to think about how you will put your learning into practice and the effect that you intend it to have on yourself, clients or pupils and possibly your colleagues. Thinking through the methods you will use – for example, further reflection, feedback from your clients or pupils and colleagues, discussion with your line-manager, data on client/pupil destinations, etc. – will enable you to plan in the time to do this and record your findings. These findings will then feed in to your next CPD cycle.

If you are employed, your employer is likely to have a system for planning your CPD. Alternatively, professional bodies provide systems that can be used by their members. Before you actually undertake a CPD activity it can be useful to look back at your plan to remind yourself of the reasons for undertaking the CPD and what you hope to gain from it. Once you have undertaken the CPD you should record that it has taken place and how long you spent on it. This is important if your professional registration depends on undertaking so many hours' CPD each year.

Reflection and recording

> *How noble and good everyone could be if, every evening before falling asleep, they were to recall to their minds the events of the whole day and consider exactly what has been good and bad. Then without realizing it, you try to improve yourself at the start of each new day.*
>
> *Anne Frank,* Diary of a Young Girl

Reflection on your CPD should be two-fold.

Firstly, a reflection on how well the CPD met your identified needs and preferred method and style of learning. Reflecting on this will help you to understand what suits you and show that you have spent your time and money wisely.

Some people find it useful to write themselves an action plan at the end of a CPD activity to summarise what they have learned and how they will put this into practice and the potential benefits to their clients, colleagues and organisation. This can help to reinforce the learning and can be especially useful if shared with a colleague with whom a future discussion can be held on the actual impact of the activity.

Secondly, you need to reflect on the impact the CPD has had on your professional practice and any impact on your clients/pupils and colleagues. This may not happen immediately but scheduling in time for this reflection as part of your CPD planning will mean that you can reflect fully on the impact that your CPD has had.

The act of writing this down helps with the reflection as well as meeting professional registration requirements that require reflection on the impact of your CPD. Time spent on this reflection and thinking through how you will or have put your learning into practice and what will change or has changed about your practice, can also count towards your CPD hours for many professional bodies.

Doing this type of reflection about a course you have attended is quite straightforward. However, as mentioned earlier, there are many different types of CPD, even unplanned things. For example, keeping notes from what you have learned at team meetings, network meetings, conversations with colleagues, etc. can contribute to your overall CPD, and if reflected upon fully as regards its actual impact can also count towards CPD hours. We look at reflection in more detail in Chapter 4.

Training organised by your employer that is compulsory for everyone to attend can also count as CPD even though you have not determined the need for this yourself. Even if you feel that this is 'sheep-dipping' you can prepare for it by thinking through how it will meet your own professional needs and how you will use it and measure its impact on your practice. Thinking through who else will be attending the training and making a point of networking with fellow delegates who can help to develop your knowledge is also time well spent. Work-based CPD is often a way of meeting up with colleagues, which in itself can also be a useful CPD activity.

Being able to look back at your CPD plans and what you have achieved over the course of a year is also valuable as it can serve to motivate you and increase your self-confidence. If you look back over a few years' worth of records you can really see the difference in terms of your own development and the ways in which you have chosen to do your CPD. You can also see if you have become stuck in a rut or if you are really embracing the opportunities available to develop your professional practice.

CPD records can also be useful when applying for new roles as they can act as a reminder of the effort you have made to maintain and develop your professional competence and the judgement and expertise you have used in deciding upon and planning how your CPD needs have been met.

Sharing

We have found that identifying opportunities to disseminate and share your learning with colleagues is a good way for both embedding your own learning and helping others to develop as well. Peer discussion can lead to further ideas for improvement as well as positive reinforcement for your own practice. In times when there is less money available for attending events and sharing practice with peers, there is a need to embrace technology for this sharing, for example, Communities of Interest or other online discussion groups, writing a report on a CPD event for a regional e-newsletter or even meeting up over a virtual breakfast or lunch to discuss what you have done as CPD over the last few months.

Reflection

The evolution of your CPD needs

Look back at the CPD you have undertaken over the last three years.

- What does this show you about the skills and knowledge you have developed?

  ____

  ____

- What does this show you about the changes in the sector?

  ____

  ____

- What does this show you about how the methods of meeting your CPD have evolved?

  ____

  ____

Self-awareness: Motivation for undertaking CPD

Look back at a recent CPD activity and ask the following questions:

- Did the CPD meet your preferred learning style?

  ____

  ____

- Did the CPD meet your preferred method of learning?

  ____

  ____

- What was your motivation for undertaking this CPD?

  ____

  ____

- How did the CPD improve your professional skills and knowledge?

  ____

  ____

- How do you know that it did? What evidence do you have?

  ____

  ____

- If you had to do this CPD again would you choose the same activity? Give reasons.

  ____

  ____

Activity

Take a look at the three professional branches in the CDI Career Development Sector Progression Pathway: Career Education; Career Guidance/Development or Career Coaching/Talent Management and locate the level of role relevant to you – www.thecdi.net/Career-Development-Sector-Progression-Pathway. This may be FC (First Contact); S (Support); P (Practitioner) M (Manager) or any of the specialist or more senior management roles.

Look at any of the National Occupational Standards: Career Development (NOS: CD) that are listed for your role and ask yourself the following.

- How well do you meet the Performance Criteria and Knowledge and Understanding Criteria?

  ____

  ____

- What are your CPD needs in relation to this NOS: CD?

  ____

  ____

- Where could you look to find information on how to meet these needs?

____

____

- If you are thinking of moving roles, what CPD activities would help you to do this?

____

____

Conclusion

In this chapter we have looked at definitions of CPD and why it is important and to whom. In an evolving sector in which there may not be as much funding for training or as much time as there once was, we have considered the ways in which CPD can be made more meaningful to you as a person and relate to your specific needs as a practitioner. We introduced the SOARS model for planning CPD and suggested that by using such a model you can identify ways to meet your own specific CPD needs, continue to provide an effective service for your clients/ pupils and future-proof yourself to meet the demands of the sector.

CPD need not be expensive; its worth may be what it cost but its value is in the way you use what you have learned.

References

Allan, G. and Moffett, J. (2015). Professionalism in career guidance and counselling – how professional do trainee career practitioners feel at the end of a postgraduate programme of study? *British Journal of Guidance & Counselling*. Published online. DOI: 10.1080/03069885.2015.1063111. Abingdon: Taylor & Francis.

Career Development Institute. (2014). *Code of Ethics*. Stourbridge: CDI. Available at: www.thecdi.net/Code-of-Ethics [Accessed 9 June, 2016].

Chartered Institute of Personnel and Development. (2016). *Continuing professional development policy*. Available at: www.cipd.co.uk/cpd/policy.aspx [Accessed 9 June, 2016].

Frank, A. (2016). Goodreads.com. www.goodreads.com/author/quotes/3720.Anne_Frank?page=2 [Accessed 9 June, 2016].

Friedman, A. (2014). *2014 Professional Body Sector Review.* Bristol: Professional Associations Research Network (PARN). Available at: www.parnglobal.com/2014-professional-body-sector-review-out-now [Accessed 9 June, 2016].

Honey and Mumford. *Learning Style Questionnaire.* Available at: http://peterhoney.com [Accessed 9 June, 2016].

International Association for Educational and Vocational Guidance (IAEVG). (1995). *Ethical Standards.* Ottawa: IAEVG. Available at: http://iaevg.net/ [Accessed 9 June, 2016].

Kumar, A. (2008). *Personal, Academic and Career Development in Higher Education: SOARing to success.* London: Routledge.

Law, B. and Watts, A.G. (1977). *Schools, Careers and Community: A Study of Some Approaches to Careers Education in Schools.* London: Church Information Office. Available at: www.hihohiho.com/memory/cafdots.pdf [Accessed 9 June, 2016].

Madden, C. and Mitchell V.A. (1993). *Professions, Standards and Competence: A Survey of Continuing Education for the Professions.* Bristol: University of Bristol.

Neary, S. (2016). Only qualifications count: Exploring perceptions of continuing professional development within the career guidance sector. *British Journal of Guidance & Counselling.* Published online. DOI: 10.1080/03069885.2016.1180665. Abingdon: Taylor & Francis.

Sadler-Smith, E., Allinson, C.W. and Hayes, J. (2000). Learning Preferences and Cognitive Style: Some Implications for Continuing Professional Development. *Management Learning* 31(2), pp.239–256.

Useful resources

If you would like to consider some of the ideas we have looked at in this chapter the following websites are worth exploring.

Association of Graduate Careers Advisory Services (AGCAS): www.agcas.org.uk

Career Development Institute: www.thecdi.net

Career Development Institute: Career Development Sector Progression Pathway: www.thecdi.net/Career-Development-Sector-Progression-Pathway

CIPD (Chartered Institute of Personnel and Development): www.cipd.co.uk/cpd/default.aspx

National Occupational Standards: Career Development: www.thecdi.net/National-Occupational-Standards

Reflection page

3 | Being a professional in the career development sector

Introduction

In a constantly evolving sector, where what career development practitioners do is often subject to changes in government policy and can at times be undervalued, it is important that we see ourselves as professionals, know what this means and are able to explain this to policymakers and the general public.

If we don't know what the profession is, why it is a profession and what our role is in its maintenance and development, then we cannot expect others to see this. Nor can we expect them to value what we do as professionals unless we maintain and develop our professional status.

The term 'professional' has many definitions, which at times can cause confusion. Should the term only apply to those with certain qualifications and who have joined a professional body? Is the term more about how you do the job rather than the job you do?

The purpose of this chapter is to try to provide some answers to these questions and to help you to think through what it is that you do that is valuable and worthy of the title professional.

This chapter is about:

- what the career development profession is
- what makes you a professional
- your professional identity
- maintaining your professional practice and status
- using and contributing to research
- the role of professional bodies
- registered professional practice
- demonstrating that you are a professional.

What is the career development profession?

What we do as career development professionals and where we do it has moved on considerably since 1902, when local education authorities and Labour Bureaux were created, and 1909, when the Labour Exchanges Act and Education (Choice of Employment) Act established the Juvenile Employment Service (Peck, 2004). Since the turn of the century, career services in the UK have experienced significant change due to privatisation, multi-professional working and workforce realignment. The introduction of work-based training routes and the plethora of different job titles have contributed to a certain lack of professional identity and confusion among practitioners, policymakers and the general public.

In *Career Guidance and Public Policy*, the Organisation for Economic Co-operation and Development (OECD) in 2004 defined **career guidance** as follows.

> *Career guidance refers to services and activities intended to assist individuals, of any age and at any point throughout their lives, to make educational, training and occupational choices and to manage their careers. Such services may be found in schools, universities and colleges, in training institutions, in public employment services, in the workplace, in the voluntary or community sector and in the private sector. The activities may take place on an individual or group basis, and may be face-to-face or at a distance (including help lines and web-based services). They include career information provision (in print, ICT-based and other forms), assessment and self-assessment tools, counselling interviews, career education programmes (to help individuals develop their self-awareness, opportunity awareness, and career management skills), taster programmes (to sample options before choosing them), work search programmes, and transition services.*

So, it was no wonder that the landscape in which these services are performed was, in 2010, described as being 'tentacular' by Dame Ruth Silver, Chair of the government-commissioned Careers Profession Task Force and the person charged with strengthening the professionalism in the sector. Her Vice Chair, Professor Rachel Mulvey explained this adjective in an article for the National Institute for Career Education and Counselling (NICEC) in 2011 saying:

> *the landscape really is very complex: it runs along a spectrum of provision from youth to any age, by way of targeted groups needing particular attention; it includes people in education – secondary, further, vocational, professional and higher and training (off and on the job) and those not in education or training with provision ranging from formal publicly funded services to informal grass roots activities either of which may experience management by target or by self-regulation.*
>
> *Mulvey (2011: 6).*

This sector complexity led the Careers Profession Task Force to make a series of recommendations which, as well as having applicability across publicly funded provision in England, which was the focus of the report, are also of relevance to career development services across the UK. The recommendations (2010) focused on the need for cohesion, increased professionalism, progression and continuous professional development across the sector, as follows.

- Establishing an overarching group of professional bodies as a single authoritative voice.
- Developing common professional standards and a common code of ethics, leading in time, to:
  - establishment of a Register of Practice for careers professionals;
  - establishing minimum entry level qualification for careers professionals of QCF Level 6;
  - a commitment to continuous professional development (CPD);
  - transition arrangements for those practising below Level 6;
  - development of a single career progression framework including a work-based route;
  - demonstration of a commitment to CPD;
  - initial training and CPD to include a focus on LMI and Science, Technology, Engineering and Mathematics (STEM); and
  - random sampling of self-declared minimum level of CPD.

Since the Careers Profession Task Force reported, in 2010, and following the work done by the Career Development Institute (CDI), much has happened to help to bring cohesiveness to the career development sector (rather than the career guidance sector) and to increase its professionalism. We now have one professional body in the CDI – the National Association for Educational Guidance for Adults, Association for Careers Education and Guidance, Institute for Career Guidance and Association of Careers Professionals International having come together in April 2013 as the CDI. This enables the profession to have a single authoritative voice when lobbying government and assemblies, and a single point of call for members to voice their views and seek support. It also provides the opportunity for everyone working in the profession to see themselves as having more in common than they have of difference.

National Occupational Standards for Career Development (NOS: CD), revised and updated by the CDI so that they cover the skills, knowledge and understanding required for all career development roles across the entire UK sector, were published in 2015 (CDI, 2015). These updated the previous NOS, which covered career guidance. The NOS: CD form the basis of the Career Development Sector Progression Pathway (2015), which shows the functions required to be performed in all levels of roles, the skills and knowledge required and the qualifications which are appropriate for each.

The pathway acknowledges the wide range of roles performed across the profession from first contact, through to support roles, practitioner, specialist practitioner, manager, senior manager and specialist roles in lecturing, consultancy, inspecting and research and the ways in which a person can progress their career. It also shows the interrelationship between the different branches of the profession: career education, career guidance/development and career coaching/talent management and the career mobility that is possible between them.

Complementing the pathway is the updated CDI Code of Ethics (2014) to which all CDI members must adhere. This details 12 ethical principles of: accessibility, accountability, autonomy, competence, confidentiality, continuous professional development, duty of care (to clients, colleagues, organisations and self), equality, impartiality, justice, transparency and trustworthiness. Taken together, the NOS: CD and the Code of Ethics show what is required for professional practice in the sector and the pathway shows the level of qualification recommended for each level of practice.

The fact that qualifications used in the pathway cover career education, career guidance, career coaching, career consultancy and talent management again helps to bring a structure to the profession and recognition of the breadth and depth of career development services on offer. Qualifications include those that are work-based as well as those studied at university, and recognise the fact that for many in the profession there is a need to provide a work-based route for progression. For those people who achieve a qualification in a career development subject that covers the relevant NOS: CD, is at least at QCF Level 6 (or SCQF Level 11 in Scotland) and is a minimum of 60 credits in size, there is the option to join the UK Register of Career Development Professionals.

The breadth of qualifications accepted for the register also extends the sector by recognising qualifications that also align with career development. This allows members of other professional associations, such as the Chartered Institute of Personnel and Development (CIPD) and the British Psychological Society (BPS), to regard themselves as part of the career development profession and join the register.

However, in spite of this work to bring cohesion to the profession, many practitioners do still feel de-professionalised. As the sector continues to progress there is the need to embrace the changes brought about by various pieces of legislation, such as in England where the Education Act (Great Britain, 2011) specifically impacted on the careers workforce for young people while at the same time a National Careers Service for adults was established.

Similarly, in Scotland, Wales and Northern Ireland, although there are all-age services these too have also been subjected to change due to evolving policy agendas, as the following examples illustrate.

- In Scotland, the development of a wider career development community was a vision of the Scottish Government Strategy for Career Information, Advice and Guidance (CIAG) published in March 2011. More recently, 'Education Working for All! Commission for Developing Scotland's Young Workforce Final Report (2014)' covers the enhancement of the relevance and quality of work experience and involvement of employers in the delivery of CIAG.
- In Northern Ireland, 'Preparing for Success 2015–2020 – A Strategy for Careers Education and Guidance' was launched in March 2016 and sets out the Department for Employment and Learning and the Department of Education's strategic vision for Careers Education and Guidance for the next five years (DELNI, 2016).
- In Wales, Careers Wales helps to develop the nation's skills base and to support the effectiveness of expenditure on education and training, thereby contributing to the economic and social well-being of Wales. The overall focus for the service is to help people secure the best career available to them. Services are delivered in relation to the ambitions set out in 'A curriculum for Wales – A curriculum for life' (Welsh Government, 2015), 'Successful Futures', the 'Skills Policy Statement' (Welsh Government, 2014) and the 'Youth Engagement and Progression Framework' (YEPF) (Welsh Government, 2013) and in the wider context the Welsh Government commitment to implementation of the Well-being of Future Generations (Wales) Act 2015.

In England the differences between the qualification levels recommended for the delivery of career guidance to young people and the qualification for the same service to adults do not help. National Careers Service contracts do not state that those offering career guidance have to hold a qualification at QCF Level 6 or above in career guidance/development. However, the 'Revised Statutory Guidance – Careers guidance and inspiration in schools' (DfE, 2015) does recommend that those providing career guidance in schools and colleges do hold such a qualification and are also on the UK Register of Career Development Professionals.

During 2016, the Government in England showed increased interest in the profession, and in March a meeting was hosted by Careers England, Careers and Enterprise Company and the Career Development Institute at which key stakeholders discussed the role of professionalism in the careers sector. Informed by a briefing paper produced by Hooley, Johnson and Neary (2016), which set out the background, evidence and key issues relating to professionalism in careers work in England, the participants discussed the key roles of career development professionals who provide career guidance in schools and career leaders responsible for the orchestration of the careers education, information and advice provision including the involvement of employers.

The fact that those who provide careers education and careers leadership in schools have a dual role adds a further dimension to the concept of professionalism, as these people are dual professionals with a need to maintain and develop their teaching role and/or management role within the school as well as the need to develop relevant skills and knowledge in career development.

These developments and the fact that there is a plethora of unprotected job titles in use, as identified in *Understanding a 'career in careers'* (Neary, Marriott and Hooley, 2014), means that the need to focus on what makes you a professional or a dual professional, how you can maintain and develop this, contribute to the body of professional knowledge and adhere to professional values and ethics becomes even more important. As is the need to be able to advocate for your profession and its connection to a community.

What makes you a professional?

There are many definitions of 'professional' as a concept and as the world of work evolves it becomes increasingly difficult to define. Usually it is defined by a set of inclusive criteria, such as qualification levels, theoretical and esoteric knowledge base, autonomous practice, etc. We are using here Evetts's (2014) description, which includes the possession of knowledge and skills that are based on a common body of theory and enacted through a recognisable set of professional practices. In the face of such fluid definitions it is key that you know how to present yourself as a professional.

The Network for Innovation in Career Guidance and Counselling in Europe (NICE) (Schiersmann et al., 2012) identified a number of ways in which being a professional can be demonstrated:

- effectively regulating relations between clients, themselves and other stakeholders (e.g. employers, policymakers, other professionals)
- building and maintaining constructive relationships
- dealing with potential role conflicts
- engaging in reflective practice
- employing critical thinking
- adopting professional values and adhering to ethical standards
- recognising the need to develop own competence continuously
- integrating current research and theory into practice
- keeping up with societal and technological developments
- publicly advocating for their profession in the interest of clients
- supporting science and policymaking in regard to their field
- respecting human rights and demonstrating openness and understanding for diversity.

These recommendations, together with a common understanding of the skills performed and knowledge required to work in the career development profession, are key to understanding what makes you a professional.

This common understanding of the skills and knowledge needed can be achieved by using the National Occupational Standards: Career Development (NOS: CD). According to the UK Commission for Employment and Skills (UKCES), National Occupational Standards are statements of the standards of performance individuals must achieve when carrying out functions in the workplace, together with specifications of the underpinning knowledge and understanding. As *standards* they are statements of effective performance which have been agreed by a representative sample of employers and other key stakeholders and approved by the UK NOS Panel. NOS are developed for employers by employers through the relevant Sector Skills Council or Standards Setting Organisation or, in the case of the NOS: CD, by the Career Development Institute as the professional body for the sector. Further information on the National Occupational Standards: Career Development is provided in Chapter 8.

The theoretical knowledge base

Having a theoretical knowledge base is often cited in definitions of a profession, one upon which expertise and practice is based. According to Williams (1998), some of the newer professions, such as teaching and social work, have sought professionalisation through a range of measures including defining a body of theoretical knowledge, extended initial training grounded in academic disciplines, all-graduate entry, removal of unqualified personnel and investment in a growing body of research and scholarship through postgraduate education, thus contributing to extending the practitioner-researcher base.

In the UK, a lack of funding to undertake research has not helped to grow the body of professional knowledge, although centres, such as the International Centre for Guidance Studies (iCeGS) at the University of Derby, postgraduate research facilities at a number of UK universities, and the work by NICEC Fellows and those who contribute to the *NICEC Journal* do mean that for those practitioners who are able to afford to undertake research the facilities to do so and means of publication are available.

However, for the majority of practitioners reliance on what they learned as part of their initial training can be the norm unless time and effort are devoted to keeping up to date with the latest research or undertaking some research themselves. Neary and Hutchinson (2009) state that developing a workforce that is skilled in research methods and that can apply them in developing both their own and their organisational practice, offers the career guidance sector a new strand of professional practice through contributing to the theoretical and the applied body of knowledge.

A body of practitioners with skills, passion and the resources to undertake more practice-based research would greatly contribute to the credibility of the professional image sought by the sector as a whole. The research that is commissioned by government and public bodies is predominantly allied to policy and as such does not always facilitate the sector in growing and evolving the necessary knowledge base.

Neary and Hutchinson go on to say that the OECD report (2003) for the UK identified a strong knowledge base for careers guidance services, but noted that much of the research is insufficiently disseminated to practitioners. This has a significant impact on initial training and continuous professional development in maintaining the expert knowledge of the practitioner workforce. They further add that Kidd et al. (1994) found practitioners had only limited use for theory and that it did not apply to practice. Douglas (2004) argued that, as an element of professional development, practitioners should engage with soundly based theory as a means to stretch views and challenge practice.

As having and using a body of expert knowledge is one of the characteristics of a profession and of being a professional, then, as Irving and Marris (2002) argue, practitioners need a deeper understanding of the challenges faced by their clients and this can be gained from engagement with research activities. Undertaking this in the career development sector in the 21st century is not without its difficulties for practitioners, as in the cautionary note sounded by Bimrose (2006); Bimrose challenges the ability of practitioners to be able to deliver evidence-based practice due to the lack of freedom in exercising professional judgements as a consequence of policy constraints.

When considering theoretical knowledge, it is helpful to consider what we actually mean by theory. Theory as a word and concept may have different meanings to different people.

When you hear the word 'theory' what do you think of? Some people will say that it is:

- a set of ideas
- abstract and has nothing to do with practice
- created by academics
- complicated and difficult to understand.

We like the definition provided by Bill Law, who considers that all our practice is based on theory in some way or other.

> *Theory offers a set of descriptors of what happens, explanations, suggestions why they happen in the way they do; and predictions, anticipating what can happen in what conditions.*
>
> *(Law, 1996: 46)*

What this means quite simply is that theory is a way of trying to explain what happens in life. Douglas (2004) suggests that:

> *Theory helps us to understand complex situations that affect our work, to make sense of the issues people face, to set problems in context and to examine possible solutions.*
>
> *(Douglas, 2004: 30)*

In the career development sector, we have a number of theories that inform the basis of our practice. As part of your initial training you will have engaged with some of these, such as person-environment fit theory (e.g. Holland, 1959), structural (e.g. Roberts, 1968) and developmental (e.g. Super, 1957). Many of these original theories have been updated and other theories have been introduced that have influenced and informed our thinking about how we work with our clients. We do not plan to focus on theory here as this would fill a book in its own right. If you want to learn more about theory that supports our practice have a look at Kidd (2006), Yates (2014), and Reid (2016), which all have accessible chapters focusing on theory to support career development practice. Details of these publications can be found at the end of the chapter.

For career development to be seen as a profession and for those working in it to be acknowledged as professionals, it is vital that theory is recognised as a foundation of practice. Maintaining this standing requires a determination by all who work within the sector to not only maintain and develop the skills and knowledge required but to also contribute to and use the body of knowledge. We explore this in much more detail in Chapter 5.

Ethical practice

To quote Bananarama and Fun Boy Three, *it's not what you do but the way that you do it, that's what gets results*. Therefore, as well as maintaining and developing competence and contributing to and learning from the professional body of knowledge, the other essential part of being a professional is adherence to a code of ethics. This defines professional behaviour and serves to protect the public, the profession, and those who practise within the profession. Ethical behaviour involves incorporating the principles provided in the code of ethics into professional life and using the code to help determine a course of action.

One of the Careers Profession Task Force recommendations for the professionalisation of the career development sector was the establishment of a common code of ethics. Some of the founding bodies of the CDI had their own codes of ethics but as this was particular to one branch of the sector it was important that a Code of Ethics was produced that embraced the entire sector. This was initially published in 2012 and then revised in 2014 by the CDI.

This Code of Ethics covers the professional practice required of all CDI members working at all levels throughout the sector, recognises the diversity of their backgrounds and work settings and informs the public of the 12 ethical principles to which all CDI members adhere. The CDI also has a Discipline and Complaints procedure, which can be used when a member is thought to have been in breach of the Code. Failure to adhere to the Code of Ethics can result in expulsion from membership.

Adhering to a code of ethics is more than just signing a piece of paper to say that you will do so. It requires reflection on practice and how this has adhered to the code. This can form a key part of your continuous professional development as a professional in the sector.

Knowing how to use a code of ethics is also key to your professional status, so that when faced with an ethical dilemma you know the value of reviewing relevant professional literature, consultation with experienced colleagues, generation of potential courses of action, selection of an appropriate course, evaluation, implementation and monitoring of the outcome. Example case studies, produced by members of the CDI Professional Standards Committee, on using the Code of Ethics can be found at www.thecdi.net/Code-of-Ethics---Case-Studies.

Your professional identity

The above has shown you what the career development profession is and what being a professional should be about, but what gives you, personally, your professional identity?

Neary (2014) questioned career practitioners about how they defined their professional identity. She found that many felt this a challenging question to answer, but predominantly the answers fell into three categories; (i) emphatic: 'I am a career adviser/education adviser'; (ii) 'that would depend on who I am talking to'; and (iii) 'difficult, because I have lots of roles'. This diversity of responses suggested the multidisciplinary nature of careers development work often challenges practitioners in being able to define their professional identity.

Neary continues by saying that professional identity is the concept that describes how we perceive ourselves within our occupational context and how we communicate this to others. There are varying academic definitions of professional identity. Ibarra (1999) suggests that it evolves through work socialisation and observation of our peers; Larson (1977) argues it is based on shared expertise. Professional identity can be established and supported by the infrastructure that contributes to creating a shared sense of commonality among practitioners. Hughes (2013) presents counselling as an example of an occupation that has a clear identity because it is underpinned by a professional association, a body of knowledge, nationally recognised qualifications, a national register explicitly defining CPD requirements, client contact hours and supervision. As stated above, there has been significant work done on many of these activities by the Career Development Institute since 2013. This focus on standardised requirements for the professional will help in contributing to the establishment of the professional identity of career development practitioners.

Contributors to professional identity formation

How is professional identity developed? What contributes to practitioners as individuals feeling they have a professional identity? As can be seen from the three key responses to Neary's question, professional identity may mean different things to different careers practitioners. For many, the use of job title was a determinant in defining who they were professionally. Those defining themselves through a job title often felt they had a stronger professional identity than those whose job title was perceived to lack clarity.

Certain changes in job titles, such as the change from 'careers adviser' to 'personal adviser' and the introduction of the generic term 'information, advice and guidance' (IAG), influenced how many practitioners perceived themselves. It was important to practitioners that their job title described what they did; job titles that were vague or indistinct were felt to impact both on how practitioners perceived themselves and how they felt perceived by others. Hence, the response of 'that would depend on who I am talking to' by practitioners who felt they had to customise the description of their job role for different audiences.

Job titles therefore have an important role. They support practitioners to articulate what they do, often identifying an area of specialism: 'young people', 'adult' or 'higher education'. The use of 'careers adviser' in a job title was perceived to have a higher professional status than a more generic term such as 'IAG adviser' or 'personal adviser'.

The second factor contributing to professional identity for Neary's study participants was engagement in continuous professional development (CPD). All were engaged in a postgraduate qualification that focused on developing their knowledge of research, theory and policy within careers guidance. This supported participants to engage with their practice at a higher level while advancing their knowledge and academic skills.

There were varying motivations for choosing to engage in CPD of this nature; these included career progression, a perceived lack of CPD offered by the employers, and wanting to engage in theory as this was an area missing in their initial training. Taking responsibility and owning their CPD was an important element for participants, particularly when contrasted with the CPD provided by their employers, which they identified as focusing on processes and contractual compliance.

Engagement with CPD at this level contributed to some participants regaining or finding a professional identity or defining themselves as a professional for the first time. The study contributed to this through providing an intellectual engagement (some felt this was currently missing from their job), engagement with theory, exposure to policy, and an opportunity for structured reflection and to undertake research into their professional practice.

Professional identity is not static but fluid; it is strongly influenced by how we see ourselves, how we perceive others perceive us, and how we are viewed by society at large: Beijaard et al. (2004). Neary's research provides a snapshot into the views of a small discrete group of practitioners, but it suggests that what we call ourselves and how we communicate this defines who we are professionally. Equally important is that, through investing in ourselves by engaging in professional development, we take ownership of our professionalism. This is potentially what defines a person as being a professional.

Reflection

- What gives you your professional identity?

  ____

  ____

- What are your motives for doing your job?

  ____

  ____

- What are your motives for undertaking CPD?

  ____

  ____

Reflection

If you originally qualified as a teacher or in a different profession and are now working in a careers role:

- what gives you your professional identity?

  ____

  ____

- do you identify more with your original role?

  ____

  - Why or why not?

    ____

    ____

- what would help you to identify yourself more with a career development role?

  ____

  ____

Maintaining your professional practice and status

Continuous professional development is one of the cornerstones of being a professional. How can CPD help you to maintain your professional status? Looking at your CPD under the following five headings can help you to think through how your CPD can contribute to both your professional practice and your professional status.

1. How do you maintain and develop your professional skills and knowledge? (If you have a dual role, how do you do both and does one take precedence over the other and, if so, why?)
2. How do you know that you adhere to your professional code of ethics?
3. How well do you understand the career development profession, its impact and value?
4. How do you articulate the value of the profession to others in your community?
5. How do you use and contribute to the body of professional knowledge?

The following are suggestions on what can be done to achieve the above and to which you can add your own ideas.

1. Using any of the National Occupational Standards: Career Development (NOS: CD), which are standardised across the sector in the UK, you can benchmark your own practice and determine which aspects of your own skills and knowledge require development. Similarly, you could use the NICE Competences, IAEVG Competency Framework or the Institute of Career Certification International (ICCI) Competences.
2. Reflecting on your own work and how this adheres to a professional code of ethics allows you to think through how well you do this and to look at any areas that require improvement. Looking at ethical case studies produced by some of the professional bodies, such as the CDI, can provide ideas of what others consider to be appropriate courses of action when faced with ethical issues.

   Maintaining an understanding of what is happening in the profession by undertaking a Political, Economic, Social, Technology (PEST) analysis can help you to see what the changes are and how these may impact on your role. Face-to-face or virtual networking with colleagues, being a member of a professional body that provides regular updates about the sector, and being alert to relevant media items can all be useful sources of information and support in this regard.

   Accessing relevant research, such as 'The Economic Benefits of Career Guidance' (Hooley and Dodd 2015), will help you to understand the value and impact of the profession and help you to advocate and articulate this to others. Hooley and Dodd's research says that the individual outcomes of career guidance for individuals are a building of skills and knowledge (human capital), an increase in their network (social capital) and an ability to transition from one part of their lives to the next. These three outcomes all affect the ability of an individual to find and keep work. When individuals are in appropriate work it can have important implications for the wider economy, e.g. increased labour market participation, decreased unemployment, an enhanced skills and knowledge base, and a more flexible and mobile labour market. There are also secondary benefits, such as improved health, decreased crime, increased tax revenue, and decreased cost of benefits.

   Using such research is a powerful tool when talking to others in your community as well as to policymakers and stakeholders. As well as helping to keep the profession in the forefront of the minds of those who fund provision, having this knowledge is a powerful reinforcement to you of the value of what you do personally in your professional role.

3. As career development services do not exist in isolation, it is also important to consider the networks in which you operate and to analyse the benefits that the services in your network bring to you and also what your contribution is. Thinking through what the impact on the network and its clients would be if career development services were withdrawn can help you to crystallise the value of what you offer.

   If one of your network colleagues had to describe what it is that career development brings to the network, what would they say? What would you hope that they would say? Would these two things be different? Answering such questions can help you to consider ways in which you can promote the profession and your role within it.
4. Reflecting on how you use the body of professional knowledge requires knowing what this is. Professional qualifications cover a great deal of this but, as we said earlier in this book, gaining a qualification is only the start of the journey. The body of knowledge is continually evolving, and keeping up to date with developments is a key part of being a professional; equally, it can be argued, so is contributing to it. Chapter 5 on action research provides valuable information on how you can do this.

Using and contributing to research

Using the body of professional knowledge to inform practice and, in turn, using practice to inform the knowledge base, is common among professions. For example, in 2004 the Youth Justice Board looked at the research that had been undertaken in the youth justice sector into what worked in helping to reduce the likelihood of young people offending/re-offending. This led to publication of a series of 15 'Key Elements of Effective Practice', which described the basic features of effective practice and a series of companion 'Readers', which provided further information for developing deeper understanding of what constitutes effective practice in a particular area.

Having something similar for each of the 17 National Occupational Standards: Career Development (NOS: CD) would be a useful development for the profession and would provide further evidence of the value of the profession and how it works. However, looking at your own work and reading relevant information from research, and distilling from this what works and how you personally have demonstrated this in your practice or could do so, is a step towards establishing your own key elements of effective practice. Writing about this as an 'Effective Practice Case Study' and then sharing it would, in turn, contribute to the body of knowledge about the profession.

Activity

Using the following headings, reflect on a piece of your practice.

- Describe what you did.

  ____

  ____

- Explain why you chose to do the work in this way (e.g. influence of previous experience, learning or research).

  ____

  ____

- What was the outcome of this (in terms of benefit to the client, group or organisation)?

  ____

  ____

- What were the benefits to society and/or the economy of this work?

  ____

  ____

- Look at some current research in this area – does what you have read influence your thinking about how you would do the same work in the future?

  ____

  ____

- What will you do to share this learning with others?

  ____

  ____

Encouraging the continuing development of a culture where practitioners in the career development profession use and contribute to the body of professional knowledge is important. Neary and Hutchinson (2009) mention Jackson (1998), who presented a set of

12 recommendations to establish and grow a research culture within the career guidance community; the aim being to enhance theory, networks and widen the dissemination of research.

Since then, there have been a number of initiatives that have sought to engage practitioners more fully in establishing a practitioner-focused research culture.

- The establishment in 1998 of the International Centre for Guidance Studies (iCeGS). The centre has particular expertise in career guidance and career development and conducts research, provides consultancy to the career sector, offers a range of training and delivers a number of accredited learning programmes up to and including doctoral level.
- The National Guidance Research Forum (NGRF), which facilitates knowledge sharing and professional development, together with labour market information (LMI) for those interested in career guidance research and practice, including practitioners, policymakers, researchers, guidance trainees, tutors and trainers.
- The National Institute for Career Education and Counselling (NICEC) was originally founded as a research institute in 1975. It now plays the role of a learned society for reflective practitioners in the broad field of career education, career guidance/counselling and career development. This includes individuals whose primary role relates to research, policy, consultancy, scholarship, service delivery or management. NICEC seeks to foster dialogue and innovation between these areas through events, networking, publications and projects.
- Promotion and recognition of research activities through award schemes, e.g. UK Career Development Awards (CDI).
- Establishment of research communities, e.g. the CDI has a virtual Community of Interest for Career Development Research, and there are other virtual groups such as Career Debate.
- Dissemination of research activities through focused conferences and symposia, e.g. CDI/NICEC and iCeGS.
- Development of new higher-level qualifications specifically for career development practitioners.
- Practitioner-focused research publications, e.g. the *NICEC Journal* and *British Journal of Guidance & Counselling.*

As the career development sector continues to strengthen its professional status, the need to maintain and develop the research base becomes increasingly more vital, as not only does it help to improve our work with clients but also provides evidence of the impact of what we do, which is needed when persuading policymakers of the value of the profession. Knowing how to use and contribute to the body of knowledge is the responsibility of all who work in the profession and must not be seen as the sole preserve of academics.

The role of professional bodies

All of the above would suggest that there is a lot to do in order to acquire, develop and maintain your professional status and to promote the career development sector as a profession. Being a member of a relevant professional body can help you to do this. Friedman (2014) states that professional bodies perform diffuse and extremely important roles in modern societies by:

- *creating and disseminating the knowledge base on which professional practice rests through the production of magazines, newsletters, journals and technical papers*

- *defining, developing and maintaining standards of knowledge and applying that knowledge to practice in an ethical manner, as well as organising for the incorporation of new knowledge, arising from practice, to influence those standards*

- *qualifying new entrants into the profession through directly awarding, or by accrediting others to provide, education and practice supervision to meet standards*

- *taking an increasingly active role in ensuring practitioners keep up to date and develop their technical and ethical competence through CPD*

- *guarding against incompetence, incapacity and unethical behaviour through complaints and disciplinary procedures as well as through qualification and CPD processes*

- *raising the profile of the professions that they are associated with as well as their profiles by linking with other stakeholders and maintaining a presence in government circles and with the media.*

In choosing a professional body to join it would be wise to consider the above and examine how well a particular body meets these roles.

Activity

Look at the websites of the relevant professional bodies for your nation and see how they measure up to the above list.

Registered professional practice

At the start of this chapter we said that the term professional can cause confusion. Anyone working in the sector, irrespective of the level of role or qualification held, can be a professional provided that this status is earned and maintained. Where a distinction can be drawn is when a person is called a registered professional. This requires the person to hold a specified qualification of at least graduate level, to adhere to a code of ethics and to undertake a minimum number of hours of CPD per year. In the career development profession, being on the UK Register of Career Development Professionals acts as an assurance to clients and stakeholders of the career development services provided. For a profession that is yet to achieve chartered status, this acts as the professional equivalent.

To achieve a royal charter a professional body must represent a unique field of activity that is not covered by other professional bodies and at least 75% of the 5,000 required members should be qualified to first-degree level. Having chartered status confers increased status and standing from within the profession and outside in the wider world. Chartered bodies can grant chartered status to members and this provides increased individual professional status, for example, Chartered Surveyor or Chartered Accountant.

Activity

How can you develop your professional self?

	What do you do now to:	What could you do in the future to:
maintain and update your skills and knowledge?		
reflect on your adherence to and understanding of your professional code of ethics?		
keep abreast of Political, Economic, Social and Technological (PEST) developments in the profession?		
advocate for having a career development profession?		
use and add to the body of professional knowledge?		

Demonstrating that you are a professional – a call to arms

The fact that the career development profession in the UK is not yet chartered can be a source of disappointment, and to some people this can seem that they are not a true professional in the eyes of the public. However, if we compare ourselves with other roles that are chartered, how do we fare?

Activity

On page 38, we used the NICE ways of demonstrating being a professional.

For each of their criteria think how you demonstrate these; then consider a chartered profession, e.g. engineer, accountant or lawyer, and consider how these people demonstrate the criteria:

- effectively regulating relations between clients, themselves and other stakeholders (e.g. employers, policymakers, other professionals)

  You ____________________

  Other chartered profession____________________

- building and maintaining constructive relationships

  You ____________________

  Other chartered profession____________________

- dealing with potential role conflicts

  You ____________________

  Other chartered profession____________________

- engaging in reflective practice

  You ____________________

  Other chartered profession____________________

- employing critical thinking

  You ____________________

  Other chartered profession____________________

- adopting professional values and adhering to ethical standards

  You ____

  Other chartered profession______________________________

- recognising the need to develop own competence continuously

  You ____

  Other chartered profession______________________________

- integrating current research and theory into practice

  You ____

  Other chartered profession______________________________

- keeping up with societal and technological developments

  You ____

  Other chartered profession______________________________

- publicly advocating for their profession in the interest of clients

  You ____

  Other chartered profession______________________________

- supporting science and policymaking in regard to their field

  You ____

  Other chartered profession______________________________

- respecting human rights and demonstrating openness and understanding for diversity

  You ____

  Other chartered profession______________________________

- common understanding of the skills performed and knowledge required to work in the profession.

  You ____

  Other chartered profession______________________________

Hopefully, by doing this activity you will see that the career development profession has much in common with other professions. However, we do need to see ourselves as professionals and to be able to articulate why we are.

Having read this chapter, if someone asks you what you do for a living, what would you say? How you describe what you do is a powerful way of promoting the career development profession and your professional role within it. Simply saying that 'I help young people or adults to decide on what career to follow' may well be true but is also doing yourself a disservice.

In the research undertaken by Neary mentioned above, she emphasises the key components that contribute to professional identity:

Self-image: how the professional sees him/herself influences practice and their view of professional change

Role: how the professional defines it to others

Conceptions and expectations of others: what others think that the professional role does.

These three components suggest that how we see ourselves is related to both our role and the expectations of others in relation to that role. The concepts are interrelated. If we present our roles negatively or undermine our role/s then we contribute to the broader negative images of who we are and what we do. Potentially this can then influence our own self-image negatively and the external image we present to stakeholders, clients and policymakers.

As we said in Chapter 1, the range of activities that careers professionals are engaged in has broadened over recent years and is now defined in the National Occupational Standards: Career Development (NOS: CD). Recent work at a European level has helped to clarify these roles and to communicate them in an accessible way. The Network for Innovation in Career Guidance and Counselling in Europe (NICE) (Schiersmann et al., 2012) has set out a typology of the activities that comprise the skill base of the careers professional. This is conceptualised as five distinct roles that a professional may combine or specialise in.

a. **Career information and assessment expert.** Helping individuals to assess their own strengths and connect them meaningfully to the labour market and the education system.
b. **Career educator**. Using pedagogic approaches to develop individuals' career management skills.
c. **Career counsellor**. Using counselling and advice work approaches to help individuals to understand their situation and to progress in the labour market and education system.

d. **Programme and service manager**. Working with individuals and organisations to design and deliver career development programmes.
e. **Social systems intervener and developer**. Using networking, consultancy and advocacy skills to develop organisations and systems and helping individuals to succeed within them.

Activity

An 'elevator speech' is a brief pitch designed to gain support for a proposition; it is argued that it should be possible to condense a proposal to the length of a 30-second journey in a lift. Try and create an elevator speech for any of the following.

- Why should the career development profession be valued and maintained?
- What makes you a professional?
- Having read the NICE roles on page 54 and above, describe what you do for a living.

Conclusion

In this chapter we have looked at what the career development profession is, what makes you a professional, your professional identity and how you can maintain your professional practice and status. As a profession, career development professionals need to present a consistent definition of who we are and what we offer; this will then help us all to advocate for the powerful and important work that we do. Our role is increasingly important as the world of work and learning becomes broader and more globalised. Career development professionals offer a unique service that supports people in navigating the complexity of modern life, enabling them to achieve their potential. The level of understanding about our professional roles may not be as clear as it is for doctors, engineers or lawyers, but we all have responsibility for shaping our individual and collective professional identity. Every time we explain what we do, we contribute to shaping external perceptions and expectations of our role. It is up to each of us individually to take responsibility for promoting the career development profession and what being a professional means.

References

Beijaard, D., Verloop, N. and Vermunt, J. (2004). Reconsidering research on teachers' professional identity. *Teaching and Teacher Education*, 20(2), pp.107–128.

Bimrose, J. (2006). The Changing Context of Career Practice: Guidance, Counselling or Coaching? Derby: Centre for Guidance Studies.

Career Development Institute. (2015). *Career Development Progression Pathway*. Stourbridge: CDI. Available at: www.thecdi.net/Career-Development-Sector-Progression-Pathway [Accessed 9 June, 2016].

Career Development Institute. (2014). *Code of Ethics*. Stourbridge: CDI. Available at: www.thecdi.net/Code-of-Ethics---Case-Studies [Accessed 9 June, 2016].

Career Development Institute. (2015). *National Occupational Standards: Career Development*. Stourbridge: CDI. Available at: www.thecdi.net/National-Occupational-Standards [Accessed 9 June, 2016].

Careers Profession Task Force. (2010). *Towards a strong careers profession*. Runcorn: Department for Education.

Department for Education. (2015). *Careers guidance and inspiration in schools*. London: DfE. Available at www.gov.uk/government/uploads/system/uploads/attachment_data/file/440795/Careers_Guidance_Schools_Guidance.pdf [Accessed 15 September, 2016].

Department for Employment and Learning. (2016). *Preparing for Success 2015–2020: A Strategy for Careers Education and Guidance*. Belfast: DELNI. Available at: www.education-ni.gov.uk/sites/default/files/publications/de/Careers-strategy.pdf [Accessed 9 June, 2016].

Douglas, F. (2004). Thinking allowed: Developing Informed Practice. In: H. Reid and J. Bimrose (eds), *Constructing the future: Reflection on practice*. Stourbridge: Institute of Career Guidance.

Evetts, J. (2014). The concept of professionalism: Professional work, professional practice and learning. In: S. Billett, C. Harteis, H. Gruber (eds.), *International Handbook of Research in Professional and Practice-based Learning*. Dordrecht: Springer.

Friedman, A. (2014). *2014 Professional Body Sector Review*. Bristol: Professional Associations Research Network (PARN). Available at: www.parnglobal.com/2014-professional-body-sector-review-out-now [Accessed 9 June, 2016].

Great Britain. (2011). Education Act 2011, Chapter 21. London: TSO.

Holland, J. (1959). A theory of vocational choice. *Journal of Counseling Psychology*, 6(1), pp.35–45.

Hooley, T. and Dodd, V. (2015). The economic benefits of career guidance. Careers England.

Hooley, T., Johnson, C. and Neary, S. (2016). Professionalism in Careers. Careers England and the Career Development Institute. Available at: http://derby.openrepository.com/derby/bitstream/10545/601198/1/CDI+and+Careers+England+-+Professionalism+in+careers+-+March+2016.pdf [Accessed 9 June, 2016].

Hughes, D. (2013). An expanded model of careers professional identity: time for change? *British Journal of Guidance & Counselling*, 41(1), pp.58–68.

Ibarra. H. (1999). Provisional Selves: Experimenting with Image and Identity in Professional Adaptation. *Administrative Science Quarterly*, 44(4), pp.764–791

Irving. B.A. and Marris, L. (2002). A context for Connexions. In: H. Reid and J. Bimrose (eds) *Constructing the future: Social Inclusion: Policy and practice.* Stourbridge: Institute of Career Guidance.

Jackson, C. (1998). *Developing a Research Culture in Career Education and Guidance.* Cambridge: CRAC/NICEC.

Kidd, J., Killeen J., Jarvis, J. and Offer, M. (1994). Is guidance an applied science?: The role of theory in the careers guidance interview. *British Journal of Guidance & Counselling*, 22(3), pp.385–403.

Kidd, J. (2006). *Understanding Career Counselling.* London: Sage.

Larson, M. (1977). *The Rise of Professionalism.* Berkeley: University of California Press.

Law, B. (1996). A career learning theory. In: A.G. Watts, B. Law, J. Killeen, J. Kidd and R. Hawthorn (eds), *Rethinking Careers Education and Guidance.* London: Routledge.

Mulvey, R. (2011). The Careers Profession Task Force: Vice Chair's Perspective. *Journal of the National Institute for Career Education and Counselling*, 27(1), pp.3–7.

Neary, S. and Hutchinson, J. (2009). More questions than answers: The role of practitioner research in professional practice. In: H. Reid, ed., *Constructing the Future: Career Guidance for Changing Contexts.* Stourbridge: Institute of Career Guidance. pp.42–50.

Neary, S. (2014). Reclaiming professional identity through postgraduate professional development: careers practitioners reclaiming their professional selves. *British Journal of Guidance & Counselling,* 42(2), pp.199–210.

Neary, S., Marriott, J. and Hooley, T. (2014). Understanding a 'career in careers': Learning from an analysis of current job and person specifications. Derby: International Centre for Guidance Studies.

Organisation for Economic Co-operation and Development (OECD). (2003). United Kingdom Country Note. In: *OECD Review of Career Guidance Policies*. Paris: OECD.

Organisation for Economic Co-operation and Development (OECD). (2004). *Career Guidance and Public Policy: Bridging the Gap*. Paris: OECD. DOI: http://dx.doi.org/10.1787/9789264105669-en. Available at: www.oecd.org/edu/innovation-education/34050171.pdf [Accessed 15 September, 2016].

Peck, D. (2004). *Careers Service, History, Policy and Practice in the United Kingdom*. London: RoutledgeFalmer.

Reid, H. (2016). *Introduction to Career Counselling and Coaching*. London: Sage.

Roberts, K. (1968). The Entry into Employment: An Approach Towards a Central Theory. *Sociological Review*, 16(2), pp.165–184.

Schiersmann, C., Ertelt, B.J., Katsorov, J., Mulvey, R., Reid, H. and Weber, P. (Eds). (2012). *NICE Handbook for the Academic Training of Career Guidance and Counselling Professionals*. Heidelberg: Heidelberg University. Available at: www.nice-network.eu/wp-content/uploads/2015/11/NICE_Handbook_full_version_online.pdf [Accessed 9 June, 2016].

The Scottish Government. (2011). *Career Information, Advice and Guidance in Scotland*. Available at: www.gov.scot/Resource/Doc/344766/0114737.pdf [Accessed 9 June, 2016].

The Scottish Government. (2014). *Education Working for All! Commission for Developing Scotland's Young Workforce Final Report*. Available at: www.gov.scot/Publications/2014/06/4089 [Accessed 9 June, 2016].

Stephenson, M., Giller, H. and Brown, S. (2007). *Effective Practice in Youth Justice*. Cullompton: Willan Publishing.

Super, D.E. (1957). *The Psychology of Careers*. New York: Harper and Row.

Welsh Government. (2016). *Career Choices Dewis Gyrfa (CCDG): Remit and Priorities 2016–17*. Available at: http://gov.wales/docs/dcells/publications/160330-ccdg-remit-letter-2016-17-en.pdf [Accessed 9 June, 2016].

Welsh Government. (2014). *Policy statement on skills*. Cardiff: Department for Education and Skills. Available at: http://gov.wales/docs/dcells/publications/140129-policy-statement-on-skills-en.pdf [Accessed 9 June, 2016].

Welsh Government. (2015). *Qualified for Life. A curriculum for Wales – a curriculum for life*. Cardiff: Education and Public Services Group. Available at: http://gov.wales/docs/dcells/publications/151021-a-curriculum-for-wales-a-curriculum-for-life-en.pdf [Accessed 9 June, 2016].

Welsh Government. (2013). *Youth engagement and progression framework*. Cardiff: Department for Education and Skills. Available at: http://gov.wales/docs/dcells/publications/131007-yeframework-implementation-plan-en.pdf [Accessed 9 June, 2016].

Williams, J. (1998). What is a profession? Experience versus expertise. In: R. Edwards, R. Harrison, and A. Tait (eds), *Telling Tales: Perspectives on Guidance and Counselling in Learning*. London: Routledge.

Wood, I. (2013). *Commission for Developing Scotland's Young Workforce: Interim report*. Edinburgh: The Scottish Government. Available at: www.gov.scot/Resource/0043/00433287.pdf [Accessed 9 June, 2016].

Yates, J. (2014). *The Career Coaching Handbook*. London: Routledge.

Useful resources

Additional resources that you might find helpful in exploring further some of the topics considered in this chapter can be found below.

Association of Graduate Careers Advisory Services (AGCAS): www.agcas.org.uk

Bill Law's career-learning café: www.hihohiho.com

Career Development Institute (CDI): www.thecdi.net

Institute of Career Certification International (ICCI): http://iccicertification.org

International Association for Educational and Vocational Guidance (IAEVG): http://iaevg.net/iaevg.org/IAEVG/index00a8.html?lang=2

International Centre for Guidance Studies (iCeGS): www.derby.ac.uk/research/icegs

National Guidance Research Forum (NGRF): www2.warwick.ac.uk/fac/soc/ier/ngrf/about

UK Commission for Employment and Skills (UKCES): www.gov.uk/government/organisations/uk-commission-for-employment-and-skills

Reflection page

4 | Reflecting on practice

Introduction

In this chapter we will be exploring the role of reflection and reflective practice to support professional practice. Specifically, we will be considering:

- what reflective practice is
- how it supports professional practice
- the types of models and approaches that can be used to help you learn from your own practice every day.

This chapter will also be useful to anyone studying a qualification in career development at any level, as well as to practitioners at any stage of their career who wish to refresh their thinking about reflective practice.

What is reflection?

A key focus for professional practice is the importance of reflection and being a reflective practitioner. That said, reflective practice is often a term that is used with an expectation that individuals will have a common understanding about what it means. However, often practitioners are confused or unsure about what it really means to reflect on practice, why you should do it, how you might do it and what you do with what you learn! Basically, reflection is a process that we apply within our lives as well as our work to help us learn.

We are told that it is important to learn from our mistakes – that by learning from our mistakes we will be prepared next time, as we will know what worked and what didn't. A common misapprehension is that reflection is only about learning from mistakes, and although it is important that we recognise when things don't work, reflection is much more than this. Reflection is about reviewing our practice to help us learn from what works and what doesn't. But also, reflection helps us to think about what we have done and why we made the choices that we made.

Reflection is often referred to within the literature as a core element of professional practice; however, Boud et al. (1985) query the extent to which reflection is acted on by professionals. When considering informal CPD in the form of reflection, Friedman and Phillips (2004) deduce from their study the importance of the reflective practitioner and that reflection should be integral within all CPD programmes and policies.

Harrison et al. (2001) and Mulvey (2004) have made the links with concrete examples of reflection contributing to professional development activities for career practitioners. Harrison et al. specify that, within professional practice, the need to analyse and interpret situations contributes to approaches adopted. Mulvey focuses on reflective practice contributing to the virtuous circle that facilitates learning and informing future practice. Bimrose (2004) supports reflection as being of particular importance for guidance practitioners, and suggests that the issue is not a lack of interest by employers but more an inability to ring-fence time for reflection.

> *Reflection is presented as an approach to learning and professional development which allows the integration of academic knowledge with experience to produce a form of contextualized, practical knowledge.*
>
> *(Harrison et al. 2001: 205)*

Activity

When you think about reflection what does this suggest to you?

Take one minute and write down as many words/emotions that define reflection for you.

Below is a list of a few that you may have come up with. It is not definitive.

- Thinking
- Learning
- Sharing
- Observing
- Creating new ways of thinking
- Trepidation
- Awareness
- Challenging
- Uncomfortable
- Seeing
- Reacting

There are probably many more that you will have thought of, as reflection is a complex, multifaceted activity. As such, it is individual and needs to be meaningful for you. What do you want to gain from reflecting on your practice?

Roth (1989) considers reflective practice is:

- being aware of what, why and how we do things
- questioning what, why and how we and others do things
- seeking to understand underlying rationales and strategies on your own; and from others
- generating choices, options and possibilities
- viewing your own activities and results from varying perspectives
- asking 'what if …?'.

Roth suggests that reflection is about both the individual and others – reflection includes how we use others to help us learn about our practice and ourselves.

Johari window

As part of your initial training you may have come across the Johari window. This is a model that was developed by Josepth Luft and Harry Ingham in 1955 to help people to develop their self-awareness and their communication skills within a group. The model has lots of useful applications within career development work. It is also useful within reflective practice to help us think about what we know about our practice, what others might know and what skills/abilities we potentially have that we do not know about. (See Figure 4.1 on the following page.)

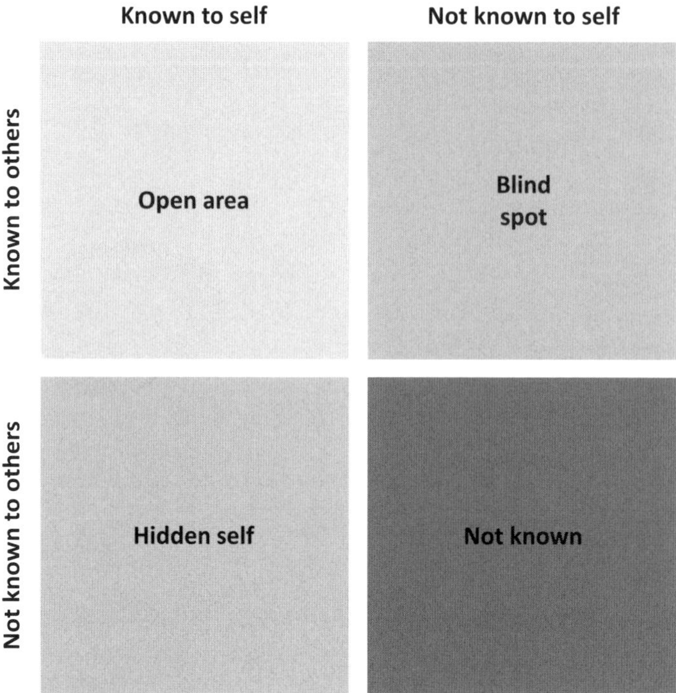

Figure 4.1: Johari window

Luft, J. (1961). The Johari Window: A graphic model of awareness in interpersonal relations. *NTL Human Relations Training* 5 (1), pp.6–7. Reproduced under a Creative Commons Attribution Public Domain Mark licence.

Think about the Johari window within the context of reflective practice.

- Window 1 – **Open area:** what you know about yourself and is known to others.
- Window 2 – **Hidden self:** what you know about yourself and you hide from others.
- Window 3 – **Blind spot:** what others know about us but we don't know.
- Window 4 – **Not known:** what is hidden from ourselves and from others.

We can learn from our colleagues to help us reflect on what we do and how we do it and we can learn about ourselves to help us extend the open areas and reduce the hidden areas and blind spots. Learning from ourselves and others is an important element of reflective practice. The Johari window provides us with a useful model to locate what we share explicitly and what we keep to ourselves.

> **Activity**
>
> Have a go at applying the Johari window to yourself.
>
> Draw a square and write the heading for each of the windows at the top.
>
> For 'Open area' and 'Hidden self' write down what you already know.
>
> For the other two areas – 'Blind spot' and 'Not known' – think about strategies you could use to address these and who might be able to help you.

Why is reflection important for professional practice?

Throughout our practice it is important that we develop our thinking, skills and practice (we talked about this in Chapter 2) to ensure that our practice grows to reflect our clients' needs. Reflective practice is one of the core competences you are expected to address in initial qualifications for all helping, career and teaching professions. For the career development sector the NOS: CD requires you to 'Reflect on, develop and maintain own skills and practice in career development'. Information about the competencies can be found in the Resources section at the end of the chapter.

There is an expectation that you develop reflection in initial training and continue to reflect throughout your career. Hazel Reid in her book *Introduction to Career Counselling and Coaching* suggests that many professions espouse reflective practice as important but do little to facilitate it. This is a valid point: as practitioners and professionals we all have the power to reflect but the level to which we engage may vary.

Reid provides a useful definition for reflective practitioners:

> *A reflective practitioner is someone who is able to research potential solutions through analysing experience and prior knowledge, in order to inform current and future practice.*
>
> *(Reid, 2016: 242)*

As a career development practitioner, you are expected to use reflection in your day-to-day work to help you build your practice.

In J.K. Rowling's *Harry Potter and The Goblet of Fire*, Dumbledore uses a 'pensieve' to help him to examine his memories; he says:

> *One simply siphons the excess thoughts from one's mind, pours them into a basin, and examines them at one's leisure. It becomes easier to spot patterns and links you understand.*
>
> *(Rowling, 2000: 591)*

This explains what we are trying to do in reflection: we are examining our thoughts, focusing on particular areas to try and see patterns to help us understand better. In the next section we start to think about the theory that underpins reflection.

Theory of reflective practice

The role of reflection in underpinning professional practice has been strongly influenced by the work of Schön (1983, 1987). Schön's representations of 'reflection-on-action' and 'reflection-in-action' have significantly influenced approaches and definitions of reflection within a professional practice context (Moon, 1999, 2004). These writers present a range of interpretations of reflection, which incorporate concepts of learning through experience, applying purpose and processing problems that appear to have no clear solution. This interpretive approach to practice supports the notion or belief in the autonomy of the professional and the view that individuals develop subjective meaning for their experiences that is used to further and enhance practice. These subjective views have been formed as a result of their experiences encountered through initial training, CPD, their area of expertise and their praxis (Eraut, 1994).

As with all the work we do in career development, reflection has a theoretical basis that underpins practice. There are, therefore, a number of theories that help us to better understand reflection and provide a structure for us to examine our practice. There are a number of theorists in this field, two of the most popular being John Dewey (1859–1952) and Donald Schön (1930–97).

John Dewey

Dewey was a philosopher, psychologist and educational reformer based in the USA. Some argue he was one of the most influential educational thinkers of the 20th century. Although he has written extensively on a broad range of topics, his work exploring the interaction between reflection and experience is what we are interested in. His seminal text on reflection is *How We Think* (1933). This book explores the relationship between thinking and learning and has influenced many other writers in the field. Dewey saw reflection as a rational, active, purposeful and linear act. He established five phases.

> 1. *Suggestions – here the mind leaps to possible solutions.*
> 2. *Intellectualisation of the difficulty in a problem that seeks a solution – this focuses on what has been directly experienced.*
> 3. *The use of a series of suggestions as a hypothesis – these guide observations in the collection of factual material.*
> 4. *Elaboration of the idea mentally.*
> 5. *Testing the hypothesis by overt or imaginative action.*
>
> (Dewey, 1933: 199–209)

These five activities provide a linear process, which in itself is one of the difficulties and challenges with the theory. It is believed by some to be too linear and mechanistic; Smith (1999) suggests that it does not consider individuals' sense of themselves or what contributes to the formation of their frames of reference. Dewey is, however, one of the initial thinkers on reflective practice and provides a theoretical starting point from which many other writers have evolved his ideas further.

Donald Schön

Donald Schön's areas of interest were philosophy, organisational learning and professional learning. In his 1983 book, *The Reflective Practitioner*, Schön examines a range of occupations including psychotherapy, science-based professions, architecture, engineering, planning, as well as identifying how senior practitioners help more junior ones. Within this context he explores 'knowing' and how professionals share and communicate this with others.

> *Practitioners themselves often reveal a capacity for reflection on their intuitive knowing in the midst of action and sometimes use this capacity to cope with unique, uncertain and conflicted situations of practice.*
>
> (Schön, 1983: viii)

What Schön is interested in is what he defines as 'reflection-on-action' and 'reflection-in-action'.

Reflection-on-action takes place after the event and is a deliberate and conscious process whereby the practitioner is retrospectively examining the situation and critically analysing and evaluating it. This process takes time and allows the practitioner to consider what they may do differently within a similar circumstance.

As career development practitioners, this is something we should do as a matter of course within our work. We need to ring-fence time to think about the activities we do with our clients and identify opportunities to improve.

> *We reflect on action, thinking back on what we have done in order to discover how our knowing-in-action may have contributed to an unexpected outcome.*
>
> *(Schön 1983: 26)*

Reflection-in-action happens during the event. It is presented as experiential reflection – almost an unconscious act – and happens in the moment of the activity. Within this mode of reflection, the practitioner is drawing on their knowledge, experience and skills to understand the situation and seek alternative strategies. Reflection happens as part of the immediate decision-making process.

Within the career development context this is something that good practitioners do quite instinctively. In one-to-one interviews, for example, you will often be making immediate decisions to take the interaction a certain way or to adopt a specific tool or strategy that you feel will work well with your client.

You will probably be using both reflection-on-action and reflection-in-action within your work. One is subconscious and happens as part of your practice. The other is a conscious attempt at reflecting on your practice and making this part of your ongoing professional development.

In the next section we will look at a number of models that will help you to apply reflection to your practice.

Models for reflecting on practice

In the last section we explored two of the most influential theorists who have helped to shape the thinking around reflection and how it can help us in developing our practice. In this section we will look at a number of models and frameworks that can structure reflective activities.

All reflective models comprise three main processes:

- retrospection: thinking back over previous events
- self-evaluation: addressing the feelings that go alongside the event
- reorientation: re-evaluating the experiences.

We are going to look at some of the key models that are helpful in exploring what we do, why we do it, how we do it and how we might enhance what we do.

Kolb's learning cycle (1984)

This was developed by David Kolb in 1984 and although originally conceived as a model that explores effective learning it has been adopted as a useful approach to reflecting on practice.

The model has four stages as can be seen from the figure below:

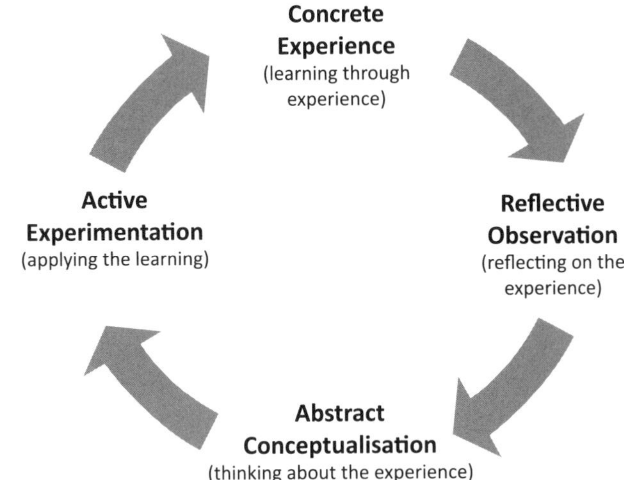

Figure 4.2: Kolb's learning cycle

(David Kolb, *Experiential Learning: Experience as the source of learning and development* (Vol. 1).)

The model can be viewed as both a cycle for learning but also as four individual learning styles. Here we are using it as a cycle for learning.

Concrete Experience: this represents engaging in the activity and having the experience. This is the 'doing' part of the model.

Reflective Observation: this is what it says it is, the reviewing or reflecting on the experience.

Abstract Conceptualisation: this stage is coming up with new ideas or ways of thinking as a result of the previous activities.

Active Experimentation: at this stage the new ideas are applied and the cycle begins again.

Activity

Use a recent experience – it could be practice-related or something else from your life – and record your responses to the questions.

- What was it about the experience that has drawn you to it?

  ____

  ____

- Why do you feel this is a good one to examine?

  ____

  ____

Reflect on/review the experience.

- What stands out about the activity for you?

  ____

  ____

- What does it tell you?

  ____

  ____

- What have you learned?

  ____

  ____

- What might you do differently next time?

  ____

  ____

- Try out the new idea. How did it work?

  ____

  ____

- What have you learned from this new approach?

  ____

  ____

The Kolb model offers a structure to think about an experience. It is both cyclical but action-orientated in that it is not just about learning from the experience, which is passive, but about how you use the learning; this makes it a dynamic approach to reflecting on practice.

This is helpful in offering a structure for reflection, but how do *you* reflect, what do *you* do?

Gibbs' model (1988)

Graham Gibbs published his 'Reflective Cycle' in 1988 in his book *Learning by Doing*. The model was developed to help people learn from situations that they regularly engage with. It was developed for teachers originally, but has been widely used by health professionals. The approach adopted is more elongated than earlier models we have explored. It is structured using a number of questions that can be used to guide the reflective approach.

1. **Describe.** It is important at the start of the reflective process to be able to articulate the situation. This allows you to identify the facts and to put boundaries on the situation. You can lay out the situation that you want to reflect on either verbally or in writing.
2. **Feel.** What were you thinking and feeling at the time? This helps you assess your emotional engagement and how this may have influenced your actions.
3. **Evaluate.** You have described the situation and considered your feelings about it, now it is important to evaluate what happened calmly and dispassionately. What was good/bad about the situation? It is important to remember that we reflect on successes as well as when things don't work as well as we wanted them to. Here we are trying to isolate the factors that contributed to what was good/bad.
4. **Analyse.** This is where you try and make sense of the situation. This is the 'so what?' point. What do your discoveries mean for your practice?
5. **Conclude.** Here you consider the options that are open to you, what actions you could have taken. What were the alternative approaches that were open to you? You might want to note all of these down and assess them individually; what might have been the consequences of each of the actions?
6. **Action.** Finally, you have to do something with what you have learned. If the situation arose again, what would you do? Which of the actions you have identified would you select and why? Once the action has been taken the process starts again! Reflection is always cyclical, as we are always reviewing and re-reviewing what we have done.

> **Activity**
>
> Identify a situation that you think might benefit from reflection. The Gibbs model works really well when reflecting on group activities, for example. If you do a lot of group work or teaching this can offer a structured approach to help you reflect. It also works well for reflection on any other types of professional practice.

Johns' model of structured reflection (2000)

This model originated in nursing practice. Christopher Johns developed the model as a way of making explicit the knowledge that is used in everyday practice. The framework aims to help practitioners to assess their reflective situation.

'Looking in' aims to centre the practitioner in terms of finding space to think and pay attention to their thoughts and feelings; this is an important element within this model. In Johns' 2013 iteration of the model, he explores this within a mindfulness context and paying attention to self within practice through becoming familiar with individual approaches to thinking and responding to situations. In this first stage, the practitioner needs to write down the thoughts that appear significant to them when reflecting on this situation.

'Looking out' requires a written description of the situation based on thoughts and emotions. Within this section there are a number of elements supported by questions. This model was originally developed for clinical practitioners; you will need to change the language to a career development practitioner and your client/customer context.

This stage is supported by a number of cue questions to help focus.

- Aesthetics (the art of what we do, our own experiences)
  - What was I trying to achieve?
  - Why did I respond as I did?
  - What were the consequences for the patient (client)?
  - How were others feeling?
  - How did you know this?
- Personal (self-awareness)
  - Why did I feel the way I did?
- Ethics (moral knowledge)
  - Did I act for the best?
  - What factors either embodied within me or embedded in the environment were influencing me?
- Empirics (scientific knowledge)
  - What knowledge did or could have informed me?

- Reflexivity
  - Does the situation connect with previous experience?
  - What would be the consequences of alternative actions for the patient (client)/others/myself?
  - How do I feel about this experience?
  - Can I support myself and others better as a consequence?
  - How 'available' am I to work with patients (clients)/families and staff to help them meet their needs?

What works well with this model is the focus on ethics. This is something that is highly important to us as career development practitioners and as such is something we need to consider. You might want to have a look at some of the ethical case studies on the CDI website to help you: www.thecdi.net/Code-of-Ethics---Case-Studies.

Additionally, the model lends itself to working with a supervisor who can guide you through some of the questions and help you to explore your responses in more detail.

Activity

You need to review the different models and possibly select different ones for different activities. It is also good practice to try different approaches to see how they work for you. All of them have different strengths and weaknesses and will support you in different ways depending on the activity that you want to reflect upon.

Reflexivity

We talk a lot in CPD about reflection but less about reflexivity. Reid (2016) discusses critical reflection and reflexive practice; she explores critical reflection, which is an awareness of the social and political context within which you practise. This is important, as reflective practice can frequently be linked to ethical practice as you may be asked to work in a way that you feel uncomfortable about or feel is contrary to your ethical framework.

Reflexivity focuses on the inner reflection and being aware of the impact of your behaviour. This is important to us as professional career development practitioners. It is not just about reviewing and reflecting on practice after the fact and learning what we might do differently next time; it is equally about acknowledging that your behaviour may be influencing how someone else may react to the situation. It is about recognising and acting on the subjective influences upon ongoing practice. Reflexivity supports us to question our assumptions, values, prejudices, actions and, particularly, how our behaviours may reinforce societal structures or organisational practice that might marginalise groups we are actually trying to help.

Finlay (2008) presents the three terms reflection, critical reflection and reflexivity on a continuum. At one end there is reflection, which focuses on thinking about an issue; critical reflection is somewhere in the middle; while reflexivity is at the other end and is dynamic self-awareness. What Finlay is trying to emphasise here is that these terms are linked but are not interchangeable. As such, reflexivity is important for recognising both the impact of practitioner behaviour on the client as well as any impacts that may affect the practitioner also.

Activity

Next time you undertake a reflective activity try and be reflexive.

Examine what contributes to and influences your practice, your values and your assumptions about yourself and others.

In the following sections we will explore a range of methods that can be adopted to support the reflective process.

Reflective writing

People like to reflect in different ways. Some people feel comfortable when thinking about things, finding a quiet place and working through a situation in their head, much like the 'looking in' stage of Johns' model. Others might reflect while they are driving home at night, before they go to sleep or when they are doing routine, household activities, such as ironing.

There are no hard and fast rules about the best way to reflect; it depends on you as an individual, your learning style and how you like to manage your life and learning. In this section we will explore different approaches. Some you may be familiar with, others you may not have tried before.

Reflective writing can be done in a variety of ways.

- Hard copy. Some people like having a notebook and pen; it is easily accessible, you can record your thoughts anywhere and it can be spontaneous.
- Electronically. There are many ways electronically for you to record your reflections. You could:

  - dictate them on your mobile phone or a dictaphone; you can play them back when you have time to listen and to think
  - write your thoughts down on your mobile phone; most smartphones have apps for a notebook function
  - use a PC or a laptop at home or work; you can set up an electronic diary and use this to record your thoughts regularly.

Learning journals/diaries

Writing down your thoughts and keeping a journal is probably one of the oldest methods of reflecting on what happens in life. There have been many great diarists, Samuel Pepys being one of the most famous. Pepys wrote a diary for over a decade from 1660, providing eyewitness accounts of historical events, including the Great Fire of London and the Great Plague. It is not expected that you write or record your daily life in a similar amount of detail, but writing down experiences you have had in order to analyse them can be helpful for reflective purposes.

Writing down anxieties or concerns can be a useful way of working through them. That is not to suggest that reflection is all about anxiety; as we have presented it, reflection is about all experiences, both positive and those that may require some development. Writing in this way is personal to you and is all about what you think. As such, this provides you with ownership and space to examine what you have done and how you might feel about it.

Barbara Bassot in her 2013 book *The Reflective Journal* has a really useful section on reflective writing where she raises a number of concerns that you might have about writing reflectively.

- What am I meant to write?
- Where do I start?
- What if I get it wrong?
- What if I write rubbish?

To help you with this, she suggests the following based on work by Bolton (2010).

> *Write whatever comes into your head, write for six minutes, don't read what you write or check it in any way, just let your writing flow. These are your thoughts and this is your writing, so it does not matter what you write. This free flow writing is a useful form of stream of consciousness, whereby all the thoughts and feelings that pass through your mind become recorded.*

Activity

Try the six-minute writing activity.

Examine how it makes you feel.

What have you found out about your thoughts on the topic you have written about?

Once you have done this try using some of the models we have discussed to help you structure your thinking and your writing.

Blogs and online reflection

Blogging has become very popular in recent years. A weblog or 'blog' is a regularly updated online journal or diary. It is often a personal website where individuals produce entries that are written conversationally. People blog on a whole range of topics, from gardening through to their favourite popstar.

Blogs can provide a useful forum for reflecting on practice, as you can write your article and those who follow your blog can post comments. This can provide a useful professional discussion forum. You may need to be careful not to disclose too much information that could compromise confidentiality though.

For those who enjoy writing in this way it can provide a refreshing and dynamic method for reflecting on practice. Even if you don't want to have your own blog, look out for other blogs that you can contribute to and comment on.

If you are interested in starting your own blog some useful advice can be found at http://blogbasics.com/what-is-a-blog/.

You may already be a member of online professional groups, such as dedicated Facebook or LinkedIn groups. These can also provide useful opportunities to share and explore your thoughts on reflective practice. Discussion forums can provide easy access to a wide range of professionals performing a similar role and having similar experiences to you. You could start a new discussion about a reflective practice topic or you could contribute to existing threads (chains of ideas).

Activity

Have a look at the discussion groups you are linked to and see how often reflective practice comes up as a topic.

You may find some existing discussions to contribute to or you can start a new one.

Feedback from others

Although reflection is a very personal activity and one that is owned by you, having feedback from others can be both useful and productive. We talked earlier about the Johari window and that you might have areas that are a blind spot, i.e. they are hidden to you but others may be aware, or they may just be unknown! Either way, you can learn a lot from others about your practice.

As part of your development you may be regularly observed. Although this can be often personally challenging, it is about helping you to see your practice from another perspective. It is meant to be purposeful and constructive. Such observations can work as a form of reflection, where you are encouraged to review your practice, both positively and developmentally, from an outside perspective.

If you do not have access to observations, you could ask a colleague (obviously with the permission of your client) to observe you. It is important that you brief them beforehand as to what you particularly want them to focus on. If they are not able to be there personally it is useful to video-record the interview or session; this way you can also reflect on the activity and share your thoughts 'after the fact' with your observer.

If you provide career development by telephone, there may be opportunities, with permission from your client, for you to digitally record the session, which again you can share with a colleague or a couple of colleagues to get their feedback on your practice. This can, of course, be intimidating and sometimes exposing at first. Some people feel they are being judged! That is not the purpose. It is a collegiate sharing activity to help you to develop and grow your practice. If no one other than your client ever sees you work how can you know you are doing well – what is your frame of reference?

Supervision

Perhaps some work you are involved in may require supervision. It is important to differentiate supervision as a supportive professional practice and one that is about managerial support.

Supervision is a common and professional requirement within counselling. All helping activities can result in practitioners feeling distressed by some of the work they do. Reid (2016) has a useful chapter that considers supervision and how it can be helpful as a reflexive process to career development professionals. Reid separates the term supervision out into 'super' – being viewed from above by someone who is experienced and has a view – and the 'vision' of the practice being observed. The purpose of supervision may vary depending on who your clients are and how you work with them. If you are habitually working with vulnerable groups you may need to access supervision.

Reid explores definitions of supervision and suggests that it is about being supportive, collaborative and learning within a culture of sharing. Many practitioners will have a colleague that they regularly meet up with and with whom they share their practice. This reciprocal arrangement can be very important, especially if you work for yourself or work in outreach and may not have much contact with a team.

If you are interested in learning more about supervision and how it can support you to develop your reflective practice, have a look at some of the suggestions in the reading list.

Strategies to support reflection

Reflection will not productively happen on its own. As a professional practice activity it is something you need to address. Below are some strategies that can help you to be more effective in reflecting on practice.

- Create time – plan to build reflective practice time into your work. You can do this with other people and introduce some of the feedback activities we have discussed.
- Move towards 'How' rather than 'Why' when you are reflecting – how might you use what you have learned? This is a proactive stance that should be adopted in all learning activities.
- Tools – try and use a tool to help you with your reflection, such as a model, diary, recording. This will help to formalise what you do; you can also refer back to it. You might want to try out different approaches to see what works best for you, or use a variety of activities regularly depending on where you are.
- Be iterative – reflections aren't a one off-activity, they are cyclical. Review what you have done as a result of the reflection and reflect on that. This will help to embed the learning.
- Disseminate your learning – find new ways (discussion groups, blogs) to share your learning and elicit feedback from others. This can also feed into self-awareness elements of CPD that we discussed in Chapter 2.

Conclusion

In this chapter we have explored reflective practice as a form of CPD. Reflection is a central component of both ethical practice and CPD – it is hard to grow and develop as a practitioner without looking at what you do. However, it is not just about looking at what you do but learning from it. We have presented a number of models that you can select to help you reflect on practice. It really does not matter which you use or how you use them, but it is important to try and find some time to think about what you do. Reflexivity is a higher-order form of reflection, but is equally important as we work in what can often be politicised environments. It is important to recognise the factors that impact on you, whether they are external, i.e. funding from organisations or individuals, or if they are internal, i.e. the values and assumptions that you may hold.

All of the activities we have identified can be used as a form of CPD. For example, if you regularly write a journal entry about your work or write a blog, this contributes to CPD.

References

Bassot, B. (2013). *The Reflective Journal.* Basingstoke: Palgrave Macmillan.

Bimrose, J. (2004). Reflection on practice: Lifelong learning for guidance. In H. Reid and J. Bimrose (eds), *Constructing the Future: Reflection on Practice.* Stourbridge: Institute of Career Guidance.

Bolton, G. (2010). *Reflective Practice: Writing and Professional Development.* 3rd ed. London: Sage.

Boud, D., Keogh, R. and Walker, D. (eds.). (1985). *Reflection: Turning Experience into Learning.* London: Kogan Page.

Dewey, J. (1933). *How We Think: A Restatement of the Relation of Reflective Thinking to the Educative Process.* Boston DC: Heath.

Eraut, M. (1994). *Developing Professional Knowledge and Competence.* London: Falmer Press.

Findley, L. (2008). Reflecting on 'Reflective Practice'. Milton Keynes: The Open University. PBPL paper 52. Available at: www.open.ac.uk/opencetl/sites/www.open.ac.uk.opencetl/files/files/ecms/web-content/Finlay-(2008)-Reflecting-on-reflective-practice-PBPL-paper-52.pdf [Accessed 9 June, 2016].

Friedman, A. and Phillips, M. (2004). Continuing professional development: Developing a vision. *Journal of Education and Work,* 17(3), pp.361–376.

Gibbs, G. (1988). *Learning by Doing.* Oxford: FEU.

Harrison, R., Edwards, R. and Brown, J. (2001). Crash test dummies or knowledgeable practitioners? Evaluating the impact of professional development. *British Journal of Guidance & Counselling,* 29(2), pp.199–211.

Johns, C. (2000 & 2013). *Becoming a Reflective Practitioner.* London: Wiley-Blackwell.

Kolb, D.A. (1984). *Experiential Learning.* Englewood Cliffs, NJ: Prentice Hall.

Luft, J. (1961). The Johari Window: A Graphic Model of Awareness in Interpersonal Relations. *NTL Human Relations Training*, 5(1), pp.6–7.
Moon, J. (1999). *Learning Journals: A handbook for reflective practice and professional development*. London: Kogan Page.
Moon, J. (2004). *A Handbook of Reflective and Experiential Learning*. London: RoutledgeFalmer.
Mulvey, R. (2004). Can I stop now? The role of continuing professional development in professional practice. In: H. Reid and J. Bimrose (eds), *Constructing the Future: Reflection on Practice*. Stourbridge: Institute of Career Guidance.
Reid, H. (2016). *Introduction to Career Counselling and Coaching*. London: Sage.
Rowling, J.K. (2000). *Harry Potter and the Goblet of Fire*. London: Bloomsbury.
Roth, R. A. (1989). Preparing the Reflective Practitioner: Transforming the Apprentice through the Dialectic. *Journal of Teacher Education*, 40(2), pp.31–35.
Schön, D. (1983). *The Reflective Practitioner*. New York: Basic Books.
Schön, D. (1987). *Educating the Reflective Practitioner*. San Francisco: Jossey-Bass.
Smith, M. (1999). Reflection, learning and education. Infed. Available at: http://infed.org/mobi/reflection-learning-and-education/ [Accessed 9 June, 2016].

Useful resources

Remember, this chapter provides a brief introduction and overview of reflecting on your practice. If you would like to explore this in more detail there are a number of good resources, including the recommendations below.

www.thecdi.net/write/Register/NOS/CDICRD02.pdf

Douglas, F. (2004). Thinking allowed: Developing informed practice. In: H. Reid, and J. Bimrose (eds), *Constructing the future: Reflection on Practice*. Stourbridge: Institute of Career Guidance.

Reid, H.L. (2013). What is supervision? In: H.L. Reid and J. Westergaard (eds), *Effective Supervision for Counsellors: an introduction*. London: Learning Matters/Sage.

Winter, D. (2012). Narrative techniques in reflective practice. *Journal of the National Institute for Careers Education and Counselling*, 28, pp.21–27. Available at: www.scribd.com/doc/90813744/Narrative-Reflective-Practice-NICECJ-28 [Accessed 9 June, 2016].

5 | Becoming a practitioner researcher

Introduction

In this chapter we explore research as a way of engaging in CPD. In particular, we focus on the opportunities and benefits of becoming a practitioner researcher. We will explore:

- how research supports the development of professional practice
- evidence-based practice and how this contributes to establishing the impact and influence of career development practice
- a model to support the implementation of research to inform practice
- opportunities for the dissemination of learning – you have done it, so now what do you do with it?

This chapter can only provide a brief introduction to some of the research skills that you can develop to help you build your practice, but we will signpost you to lots of resources that will help you develop this area of your professional practice.

Why research?

We talked in Chapter 4 about theory and how theory can support you to understand and develop your professional practice. The development of theory and practice can also be enhanced through undertaking research. But what do we mean by research?

The term 'research' can be seen as particularly formal, but you can also call it investigation, exploration, enquiry, study and examination; the terms can often be used interchangeably. For us, research is a systematic approach to solving a problem and identifying new knowledge; it is about asking questions and arriving at some conclusions. That said, much of the learning is in the journey and discovering interesting ideas as you progress through your research.

Research undertaken by Neary and Hutchinson (2009) identified a range of research activities undertaken by practitioners for different purposes. These included:

- finding out information to support clients and to be able to respond to their needs
- finding information or advice to inform practice; this might include learning how to address an issue that they were unfamiliar with
- generating a shared and balanced view of an issue at an organisational level
- pushing the boundaries of knowledge to develop new understanding.

Many practitioners are most familiar and comfortable with undertaking occupational and labour market research on behalf of their clients. While this is important, it is a well-established practice that most experienced practitioners do very well. The following activity requires you to use a wide range of skills.

Activity

Think about the research skills you have already developed through searching for and locating information on behalf of your clients.

Make a list and refer to this as you work through this chapter.

____

____

____

____

____

____

____

____

We are interested in research that contributes to developing practice and the body of knowledge that underpins and drives forward the profession. Irving and Barker (2004) suggest that:

> *Participation in research based activities should be regarded as a key aspect of personal and professional development for academic and practitioner alike.*
>
> *(2004: 69).*

Irving and Barker argue that reading research or actually getting involved in research projects can contribute to the development of new knowledge, approaches to practice, critical thinking skills and a more reflective approach to practice. Within the NICE framework (which we introduced in Chapter 1) a core competency focuses on professionalism. Within this there is a focus on cognitive resources that identify the skills and knowledge that practitioners should have. These specify: **'research theory and methods (social sciences) that test knowledge, basic statistical techniques, survey development and analysis, evaluation research and psychometric quality indicators'**. (Schiersmann et al., 2012: 76).

So, what is a researcher practitioner?

Research can be undertaken by anyone and for any reason. It might be because you are curious and questioning, or to better understand something you have observed. As practitioners we are often interested in learning about why things happen in a certain way or why a set of circumstances lead to a specific outcome. It might just be that you have noticed something new and you want to find out more about it.

Example

You are a career development practitioner working in a school. You are interested in work experience and want to find out what will help the young people you work with learn from practical work activities.

Example

You work with adults and have recently undertaken a course in cognitive behavioural therapy (CBT). You want to understand how you might use it with clients who have experienced mental health issues.

Example

You have worked in the careers sector for over twenty years and have seen much change during this time. You would like to understand how this change has been perceived by colleagues and how it has influenced practice.

Each of the above examples would lend itself to a research project that would extend the practitioner's knowledge and possibly that of their colleagues. The size of the research project would depend on the rationale for undertaking it and the resources available to support it. Some practitioners may choose to do this as a small research project that they fit around their work. Others may choose to do something more formal, for example seeking out some funding to support their study or undertake it as part of a formal qualification such as a master's or a PhD. We look at formal qualifications in a little more detail later.

Activity

Using any of the examples above or one of your own, think about what question you might set yourself and how might you answer it.

____

____

What might you do to help you answer your question?

____

____

There is a range of ways that you can approach undertaking research projects such as these. Throughout this chapter we will provide a general introduction to some. However, there are specialist skills required in research so you may want to explore this in more detail.

The National Guidance Research Forum (NGRF) has some useful information about starting research projects and developing research skills: www2.warwick.ac.uk/fac/soc/ier/ngrf/effectiveguidance/research/.

Research is fundamentally a systematic review. What you have to do/find out to answer the question you have set yourself is basically problem solving! There has been much talk in recent years about the importance of the evidence base. Undertaking research activities that contribute to furthering what we know about career development and the impacts that it might have on individuals and society contributes to building and securing the future of the profession.

Using research in your practice

As part of your initial training you will have engaged with some theory and some research about careers work. This may have focused on how people make decisions, how to structure a career development intervention, what helps build a good working relationship with a client. In fact, everything that you will have learned will be based on either research that has informed practice or evidence of observation that has produced successful outcomes.

As a professional career development practitioner, engagement in research should not end when you get the bit of paper that says you are qualified or competent to do the job. Understanding how practice is evolving and developing is a key element of continuous professional development.

Accessing research is not as daunting as it sounds. There is lots of information made available to us all the time about what works in practice; it is not all in inaccessible academic journals (although there is a lot here as well).

Research to help you develop your practice can be found in a variety of accessible ways.

Journals and publications

- CDI News via Email. In each edition of the newsletter there is a purple tab that highlights research that has recently been published. This provides a useful way of keeping up to date with research specifically relevant to the career development sector.
- *Career Matters*. Includes updates and summaries of research that may be of interest to members.
- The National Institute of Career Education and Counselling (NICEC) produces a biannual journal that includes short articles often presenting research that practitioners have been involved with.
- The CPD Resources Area of the CDI website lists a number of useful publications and online materials.

Research organisations

There is a wide range of organisations, both university-based and commercial, that undertake research aligned to the career development sector. Many organisations will make research reports available on their websites; these include:

- International Centre for Guidance Studies (iCeGS): www.derby.ac.uk/icegs
- Institute for Employment Studies (IES): www.employment-studies.co.uk/
- Warwick Institute for Employment Research: www2.warwick.ac.uk/fac/soc/ier/
- National Foundation for Educational Research: www.nfer.ac.uk/
- CFE Research: http://cfe.org.uk/
- SQW: www.sqw.co.uk

- Education and Employers: www.educationandemployers.org
- Centre for Career and Personal Development, Canterbury Christchurch University: www.canterbury.ac.uk/education/our-work/centre-for-career-and-personal-development/centre-for-career-and-personal-development.aspx.

Research commissioners

Much of the research that is undertaken is commissioned and paid for by either government or other organisations interested in learning more about a particular topic area. Often the research reports are made available to the general public through their websites; these include:

- Government departments, such as the Department for Education, Department for Business Innovation and Skills, Department for Work and Pensions and UK Commision for Employment and Skills (UKCES): www.gov.uk/government/publications.
- Cedefop (European Centre for the Development of Vocational Training): www.cedefop.europa.eu/.
- Sutton Trust: www.suttontrust.com/research.
- CIPD (Chartered Institute of Personnel and Development): www.cipd.co.uk.

Both of the above lists include just a few of the types of organisation who publish research relevant to the career development sector.

Using research

All research is undertaken for a particular reason; whether it is to find an answer to a question or to learn more about a particular topic, there is always an agenda. As such, it is important that when using research, you consider possible bias given who it was produced for and for what purpose.

Research can be useful tool to support the development of practice. Keeping up to date on what is happening in your field helps you to learn about new initiatives, policy and how practice may be developing. Research is no use unless it is used; it needs to be an active tool that raises questions and offers ideas of what can be done.

Using research in your practice helps you to understand:

- the latest theory – what is new in terms of thinking about many of the problems we are dealing with on a daily basis
- strategies and tactics – it can provide ideas about how others may have tackled similar issues as those you are experiencing
- new ways of thinking – it can be a source of motivation and ideas
- priorities – what needs to be done and why.

Activity

When was the last time you used research to inform your practice?

____

____

If you have used research, what did this do for you?

____

____

In the next section we are going to explore research that is based on practice and informs practice.

Evidence-based practice

You often hear policymakers and researchers talk about evidence-based practice, but what is it? The concept of evidence-based practice originated in medicine and is used in mental health, social work and education. It supports practitioners to build a body of knowledge through evaluating what they do in practice to identify what works and what might not work so well. This contributes to moving practice forward with evidence demonstrating how the activities may have had a positive influence.

If you want to find out more about the evidence base as a concept, we recommend Ben Goldacre's (2008) book *Bad Science*. This is a readable and funny book that focuses on medicine but provides a good introduction to issues around evidence-based policy and practice.

Policymakers are often interested in seeing 'proof' that careers work has an impact before they fund any new initiative. When they are asking for 'proof' they are really looking for a formal evidence base of research and publications that demonstrates the impact of the work that you do. This kind of formal evidence base has much more power than sharing anecdotal stories about individual clients.

Evidence-based practice according to Trinder (2000) can:

- ensure that new initiatives are likely to be successful as they have been proved in a similar context
- promote value for money as they are directly linked to practice
- empower practitioners and encourage self-directed learning for staff.

Finding and using evidence is important, but we must also remember that what works well in one setting does not always transfer directly somewhere else! Careful consideration needs to be given to contextualisation to ensure what you learn supports what you want to do. But it is also incredibly powerful to take ideas from elsewhere and adapt them to your way of working.

Tristram Hooley (2014) argues that we should actively seek out evidence for our work and contribute to growing the evidence. He suggests the following approach, which we have slightly adapted to meet the needs of a practitioner researcher.

This provides a useful approach to think about how we might engage in research as a practitioner. There are four steps in the model. These provide a process that you can follow which will broadly give you the structure of a research project. They are iterative and, as such, build a cycle of activities that can be repeated to help embed learning, similar to those we explored in the reflective practice chapter.

Some people may be interested in undertaking small research projects themselves. The next sections explore how you might start to do this. We hope to provide you with an overview of some of the issues you may need to consider if you plan to undertake research yourself.

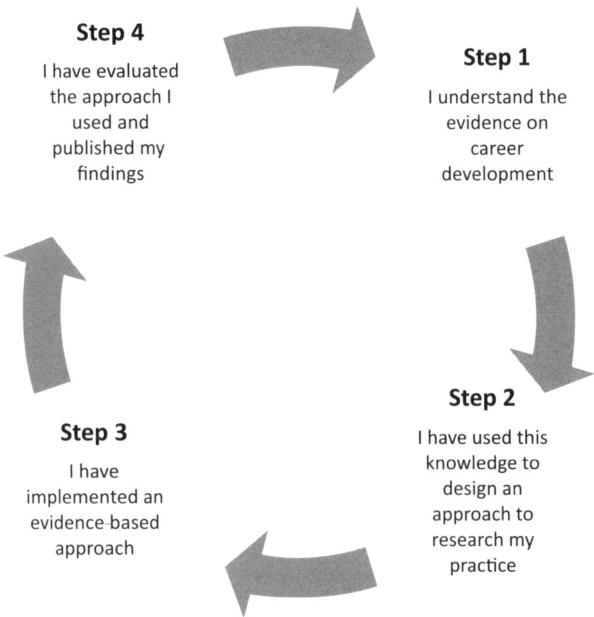

Figure 5.1: Model for evidence-based research to inform practice

Planning your research

We would recommend that you identify an area or problem that you would like to examine in relation to your practice. We have developed a template that you can use to help you think about your project; this can be found in Appendix 1. Have a look at this now and think about how you will populate it as we work through the next sections. You might want to ask yourself a few questions before you start.

- Why do you want to do this research project?
- How do you know this is an issue/problem?
- What evidence do you think you can gather?
- Who will you need to involve, i.e. colleagues, clients?
- Are there any ethical or access problems you need to consider?
- Will you be able to access some support?
- How might it inform your practice?
- How will you share your learning?

Careful planning is essential for success. Does this sound familiar? As with all journeys, you need to plan a route. This does not mean that it has to be totally prescriptive but it will help you understand what you need to do next.

Ethics

With all types of research consideration needs to be given to ethics. As career development practitioners we are familiar with the code of ethics that support and underpin our professional practice. Research is no different. You need to consider if there are any ethical issues that may affect the study you want to do.

When conducting a research project, you need to consider a number of activities to ensure your research is ethical.

- Informed consent – it is essential that those contributing to your research have been fully informed about the research, its methods and aims and what they have to do.
- Avoid coercion – there is always a power dynamic in relationships. Your clients may feel that they have to contribute. Individuals have the right to decide if they want to participate or not.
- Incentives – these can be used but they should be nominal.
- Withdrawal – you need to make sure that your participants are provided with an opportunity to withdraw if they no longer want to continue.
- Anonymity and confidentiality – ideally you will ensure that your participants cannot be identified. This may be through changing their name or the details about them. If you are working in a small organisation it is not always easy to guarantee anonymity.

- Risk assessment – there should be no physical or psychological harm to either participants or the researcher.
- Debriefing – ideally the researcher should have an opportunity to debrief the participants and to share the findings.
- Confirmation – participants should get the chance to check their narratives, especially if you have transcribed the interviews, and confirm they are happy to have their data included.

In the following sections we will explore each of the four steps outlined in the figure on page 88, and provide some ideas as to what you need to do.

Model for evidence-based research to inform practice

Step 1: I understand the evidence on career development

Before you start any research project you need to find out what is already out there. It may be that what you are interested in has already been researched and the answers are already there. Alternatively, you might find there is very little written about it. What you do find will help you to better understand your problem, inform your thinking as to what you want to explore and help you to shape your research question. It also helps to set the scene and the context for your research.

This stage of the research is usually referred to as the literature review. A literature review demonstrates that you have an understanding of the current state of knowledge for your topic area. It demonstrates that you have investigated and understand what has been written or not about the area you are interested in. It will:

- help to define your methodology or approach to research – you can see what approaches others have used to investigate areas of practice
- help to explain your findings and to compare where they may be similar or different
- demonstrate that you have an in-depth knowledge of the topic area and contribute to your expertise in the area
- be required if you want to publish in an academic journal.

Searching for literature

Searching for literature has become much simpler and easier with the internet. The problem now is more about the quantity of material available. Your role is to try and find quality literature. In the same way that you would critique occupational information, similarly you need to think about the source, age, audience, relevance to you and why the research has been done. You need to filter out literature that is useful to you and literature that is not. It is really easy to get sidetracked reading something you find interesting but not really relevant to your topic. There are a number of things you can do that will help you.

Informal searches

- Start with what you already know – there may be literature or articles that you have already read and may have initially informed your interest in the topic.
- Look at some of the sources of research we referred to in the section above on using research in your practice.
- Always check the reference list at the end of any article – this will help you to find more literature and to check the validity of what you have just read.
- Talk to people you know; they may be able to refer you to materials and resources they are familiar with.
- Consider posting a request on Twitter/Facebook/LinkedIn for recommended resources or materials on your topic area.
- Set up a Google alert – if you have a Google account you can set up an alert that will send you information on a particular topic.

Using search engines

Search engines provide access quickly to information on the internet. This can be both useful and problematic as you can find lots of information that might be relevant but at the same time much of it may be irrelevant to what you need. Think about what literature you are searching for: government reports, policy, journal articles, professional publications, newspaper/magazine articles, blogs, books? There is a lot you can find. It is important to focus your search on the topic or theme you are interested in. The key to this is using search terms; these are the phrases that you use to search the internet. Below are a few ideas that will help you with your search activities.

- Make sure you keep a record of the terms you use and the combinations you use them in. If you wanted to find out what had been written about work experience, for example, you might use the following terms: 'work experience' 'work-shadowing', 'work-based learning', 'work placement' 'young people', 'pupils', 'employers', etc.
- If you are struggling for words, use the synonym or thesaurus function in word-processing packages.
- Using quotation marks around the search terms helps to narrow the search down.
- Define a date range; you might want to set it for the last ten years, for example.

- It may be helpful to use Boolean operators in your search; this helps with exclusion of texts. The three basic operators are 'AND', 'OR' and 'NOT'. These help focus if your topic has multiple search terms e.g. 'Work experience' 'AND 'Young people' 'NOT' Placement.
- Google Scholar is useful for finding articles that are more academic: https://scholar.google.co.uk/. Here you can search for scholarly articles across different disciplines. This is important for research focusing on careers-related topics as careers research is multidisciplinary and attracts scholars from sociology, psychology, economics, and business-related disciplines.

Step 2: I have used this knowledge to design an approach to research my practice

One of the things that often puts people off research is that it is technical and has a language that is often inaccessible. This is all true! But at the same time it is unlikely that you are aiming to be a professional researcher (although you may get hooked and decide this is what you want to do). This part of the model focuses on designing the approach you will use to research your practice. Here we will look at the basics to get you started in research and guide you to some useful resources if you want to learn more.

Different styles of research collect data in different ways.

- **Quantitative research.** This focuses on things that can be precisely measured (using numbers). For example, how many clients do you see in a year, how many get jobs or training as a result of your service? To measure these factors, you might do a survey or analyse information that you collect from each of your clients. With this type of research, you can count and quantify your client group.
- **Qualitative research.** This focuses on things that you cannot count precisely and may be individual perceptions of a particular topic area. So, using a similar example, you might want to find out how people think your service has helped them. From this question you would not necessarily know how many people used the service but you might find out what they liked or disliked about it.

Each of these approaches may use different tools and methods to collect data. Mixed-method approaches tend to use a combination of both statistical and perception data.

There are many different methods for collecting data, some of which you will be familiar with – surveys and questionnaires, in-depth interviews, laboratory experiments, case studies, action research and ethnography are a few examples. There are many more that you can find out about from the resources below. It is important to select a method that helps you to answer the research question you have set for yourself; some questions will lend themselves more to one method than another. If you want to find out what people think about something, their views and perceptions, then you would use a qualitative method. If, however, you are more interested in being able to argue something statistically, you are more likely to take a quantitative approach. Information about these research tools can be found in Bell (2008).

In the next sections we are going to consider some of the most common methods used to gather research data.

Surveys

Surveys and questionnaires are one of the most popular tools for gathering data. They are usually constructed with a set of questions for the research participant to respond to. They can be delivered face-to-face, online or through self-completion. They can be used to collect both quantitative and qualitative data. They offer one of the most flexible methods for collecting both large and small amounts of data.

You need to think carefully about the type of questions that you use in a survey. Bell suggests the following types of questions.

- Open questions. These offer the opportunity to learn more about what people might think. However, people may not want to write a lot. You need to be specific in what you are asking, e.g. 'Please tell us three things you like about using self-service checkouts in a supermarket.' Everyone you ask may come up with different answers.
- Lists. Provide a selection and ask participants to select which is appropriate, e.g. list of qualifications that people may have.
- Categories. For example, age range or salary range.
- Ranking questions. Respondents are given a choice to order five listed items, e.g. 'Which type of CPD is best for you? Please rank in order from one to five (five being the lowest).'
- Scaling questions. These offer respondents the chance to rate strength of feeling or attitude (1 = strongly agree, 5 = strongly disagree), e.g. ' "I always reflect on all CPD activities I engage in." Please select which response best describes your action.'

There are a number of online survey tools that you can use to undertake a small-scale research project, such as SurveyMonkey (www.surveymonkey.co.uk) and SmartSurvey (www.smartsurvey.co.uk). Some of these provide basic free services, but others may charge a fee. Find out about any costs before you make a decision about what will be useful to you.

Interviews

Interviews are verbal and may be conducted face-to-face, by phone or through social media, such as Skype. The interview can be constructed in a number of different ways:

- structured, where there are a limited number of responses that have been previously defined by the researcher
- semi-structured, where topics have been defined but they are a prompt for the researcher to focus on what main areas need to be covered
- unstructured, where the interviewer is interested in what the respondent has to say and doesn't want to constrain them. These interviews require a lot of expertise but can provide a wealth of information.

Action research

Here we are going to focus on action research as an approach, as it links well to developing practice and reflection. This is not a method or technique in the sense of data gathering, rather it is applied research based on an identified need for a change or improvement (Bell, 2008). However, you are likely to be gathering information from different sources to help you evaluate how effective what you are doing is. Action research in the UK is specifically defined around the development of practice.

> *Action research is simply a form of self-reflective enquiry undertaken by practitioners in social situations in order to improve the rationality and justice of their own practices, their understanding of these practices, and the situations in which the practices are carried out.*
>
> *(Carr and Kemmis, 1986: 162)*

However, in other parts of the world its focus is more around social change and the gathering of information to address this. We are interested here in the development of practice but that is not to say that social change may not be an outcome of this. Jean McNiff and Jack Whitehead have written extensively on this topic and their work can be found at www.actionresearch.net.

Action research is a process of enquiry that helps you to think about and reflect on your work. It has a strong relationship with reflective practice as it is a developmental process that requires the researcher to implement an activity, then reflect on learning, then apply the learning. The Kolb model of reflective practice we looked at in Chapter 4 provides a useful framework for this. You may wish to refer back to it.

Activity

Action research project (see also Appendix 1)
You have just introduced a new feedback system for your clients. You want to find out how well this is working, using the Kolb model of 'Do, Review, Conclude and Plan':

Do – Introduce your new system.

Review – You may want to compare the level and/or quality of responses you receive now with the previous system. You may want to talk to your clients about the new approach and find out if they consider it easier to provide feedback now.

Conclude – What have you learned? Is the new system providing more/better/more useful feedback?

Plan – If you find there are other things that you can do you may want to build these into the system and start the process again.

Action research is essentially an iterative model. As such, it does not really end as you will be continuing to review what you do to find out what is working and what could be enhanced.

The above is just a brief selection of approaches that can be used to support practitioner research. There are others that you might want to explore if you are interested in learning more about research methodology. At this point you have hopefully defined the approach that you wish to use. You now need to think about how you are going to build your evidence base.

Step 3: I have implemented an evidence-based approach

In this stage of the model you are implementing your research or the practice you want to review. You need to think carefully about who you will select to partake in your research and why you think they can help you to answer your research question. Research requires transparency and clarity about the process, so you need to be clear about who you are involving and why. The implementation stage is where you are gathering your data, so it is important that you collect it from the right people in the right way. You will need to consider the ethical implications of your study.

If you are focusing on your own practice you may include yourself as one of your participants. If this is the case, refer back to Chapter 4 on reflective practice to consider methods that will help you to reflect and record your thoughts.

This step focuses on using what is already known about the activity that you are doing. If, for example, you have recently been trained in cognitive behavioural therapy (CBT), you will have not only engaged in the skill development but you will have explored studies or literature about which clients will most benefit and in what circumstances the approach is most effective. So, your research project may be to follow up on the training to build on the skills you have learned.

Example

You are finding that you are seeing an increasing number of clients who have mental health issues and you think it would enhance your practice to be able to offer them something more. You talk to colleagues who have trained in CBT and feel this might offer an interesting approach that you could use. You research who offers the training and identify an organisation that has a good track record and has been recommended by colleagues. After your training you decide you would like to test out your new skills and you want to see what difference it might make to your clients.

Within this example you would need to decide which clients you are going to work with. You may have identified a couple who you think would benefit. You will need to get consent from your client. For more on this, refer back to the section on ethics. Within this example you may choose to include yourself and, for example, record reflections of your clients after you have seen them and how you think they responded to the CBT techniques that you used.

You might also want to get feedback from your client using one of the approaches we discussed in Step 2. You might ask your client if they would be willing to complete a brief questionnaire or to answer a couple of questions about their experience. To ensure that your client can be really honest and open, you may want to ask a colleague to interview them or make sure that their questionnaire is anonymous.

In this stage of the model you are using the best evidence available to support and inform your practice. Here you are using what you have learned and reflecting on it, so you may be analysing your own behaviour and observing your client. How are they reacting to the techniques you are using? Are they appearing more positive or less negative about their particular issues? How do you know this? You might decide to use an action research approach as a structure to help you review your practice and learn about how you can best use the new skills and knowledge that you have developed.

The next stage of the model focuses on what you do with the data once you have collected it.

Step 4: I have evaluated the approach I used and published my findings

So far, you have reviewed the evidence for your study, identified the approach and the question you want to focus on, developed your research tools and implemented them with yourself, your client or others who you think can contribute to helping you understand your chosen topic.

You will have collected a lot of data by this stage, and it is likely to be in the form of narratives or numbers. You will need to consider how you are going to analyse the data you have collected. If you are collecting numerical data you are likely to be looking at producing descriptive statistics, which may be in percentages. There are a number of specialist software packages, such as Statistical Package for Social Sciences (SPSS), that can help you to undertake sophisticated analysis of your numerical data. For small projects, most people will export the data into Excel. If you used a tool such as SurveyMonkey, for example, it will automatically analyse the data for you; you can also export the data to Excel for additional analysis.

Alternatively, your data will be narrative, in which case you will be analysing it to identify patterns and themes that support the arguments. If you have recorded your interviews, you may want to transcribe them so that you have a written document to use. This is not always necessary as you may have taken in-depth notes or have written responses from the respondent. You will need to identify how often themes occur, and to do this you are likely to code your data. The code is basically a label that you use to identify a particular theme. If you undertook a literature review at the start of the process, you might have defined a series of codes that you wanted to look for in your data; alternatively, you might identify the codes when you are examining the data. Using the CBT example from page 96, if you are analysing your data about how the use of CBT is benefiting your clients you might identify that a couple of people feel more confident in how they are interacting with other people. You would then start to look for other incidences of confidence as this may be a common theme.

Once you have analysed your data, you will be able to identify your key findings. If you undertook a literature review, you can compare your findings with that of other research on similar topics. Your findings summarise what you have discovered in relation to your research question or the practice that you have been exploring.

Dissemination of learning

It is important to plan the dissemination of your research early on. This will provide you with a timeline and a goal to aim for.

Verbal dissemination

You may want to focus on presenting your research verbally.

- Workshop to colleagues as part of a staff development programme.
- Workshop to other colleagues in your network.
- Professional association event – this may be regional or national.
- Conference – again this could be local/national/international. The CDI, AGCAS (Association of Graduate Careers Advisory Services) or NICEC conferences are always good venues to reach a wide range of practitioners.

Written dissemination

There is a wide range of media that can support you to share your research.

- Blog – write a blog as part of your research so that you are sharing your experiences with others. There are many in the careers field who already do this. Have a look at Chapter 7, which explores the internet and social media.
- Organisation newsletter – you may be able to write an article for your organisational newsletter and share it with your colleagues.
- Professional association publications – you might want to write an article for the CDI publication *Career Matters* or AGCAS's *Phoenix* (the ACGAS journal) in the UK. There are a number of other professional associations in other countries that have newsletters and welcome contributions. Have a look at the newsletter for the Canadian Education and Research Institute for Counselling (CERIC), the E-zine of the Career Development Association of New Zealand (CDANZ), and the practitioner magazine of the Career Development Association of Australia (CDAA).
- Journals – you may want to write something that is aimed at researchers and others in the field. The *Journal of the National Institute for Careers Education and Counselling* is a really good starting point for this.

- Peer-reviewed journals – these are aimed at academics and researchers within the discipline. When considering peer-reviewed journals you need to make sure that you have focused your article to meet the requirements of the journal, as they focus very precisely on topic areas. You might want to consider the following: *British Journal of Guidance and Counselling, International Journal for Educational and Vocational Guidance, Australian Journal of Career Development, Career Development Quarterly* and *Career Development International.*

Writing up, publishing and presenting your research is really important. Often you learn as a result of the process of writing up your research. Tony Watts in his final lecture said:

> *My main reason for writing is simple: I do not know what I think until I have written it.*
>
> *(Watts, 2014)*

Through thinking and reflecting as we are writing we are learning. It also helps us to construct the arguments and the messages we want to promote to our audience. If you are the only one who learns anything from your research then it has a very limited impact. As a professional you have a duty to share your learning from your research and to ensure that you are contributing to the evidence base that supports our area of work.

Conclusion

This chapter has introduced the concept of the researcher practitioner. Engaging in research can have many positive effects, not just for the researcher, but also for the participants as well. Many participants often say they found that being part of a research project enhanced their confidence in themselves. You may want to get involved as a participant as well as undertaking your own research or evidence-based practice.

The model we have suggested offers a structure that will help you to explore research projects and develop the evidence base to support career development growing as an academic discipline and reinforcing the professional nature of practice. We have only been able to provide a brief introduction to the skills and knowledge to engage in research; there are many publications and websites that can help you if you are interested in pursuing this in more depth. In addition, you may be interested in undertaking a higher degree at either master's or doctoral level. These will provide you with the opportunity to engage in an in-depth research project focusing on an area you are interested in exploring further.

References

Bell, J. (2008). *Doing your Research Project.* (4th edn). Maidenhead: McGraw Hill.

Carr, W. and Kemmis, S. (1986). *Becoming Critical.* Lewes: Falmer.

Goldacre, B. (2008). *Bad Science.* London: Fourth Estate.

Hooley, T. (2014). *The Evidence Base on Lifelong Guidance.* Jyväskylä, Finland: ELGPN Tools No.3. Available at: www.elgpn.eu/publications/browse-by-language/english/elgpn-tools-no-3.-the-evidence-base-on-lifelong-guidance-extended-summary [Accessed 9 June, 2016].

Irving, B.A. and Barker, V. (2004). Living in the real world: Developing and delivering qualitative research. In H. Reid and J. Bimrose. (eds) *Constructing the Future: Reflection on Practice.* Stourbridge: Institute of Career Guidance.

Neary, S. and Hutchinson, J. (2009). More questions than answers: the role of practitioner research in professional practice. In: H.L. Reid. (ed), *Constructing the Future: Career Guidance for Changing Contexts.* Stourbridge: Institute of Career Guidance. Available at: http://derby.openrepository.com/derby/handle/10545/197210 [Accessed 9 June, 2016].

Schiersmann, C., Ertelt, B-J., Katsarov, J., Mulvey, R., Reid, H., and Weber, P. (Eds). (2012). *NICE Handbook for the Academic Training of Career Guidance and Counselling Professionals.* Heidelberg: Heidelberg University. Available at: www.nice-network.eu/wp-content/uploads/2015/11/NICE_Handbook_full_version_online.pdf [Accessed 9 June, 2016].

Trinder, L. (2000). A critical appraisal of evidence-based practice. In: L. Trinder and S. Reynolds, (eds.), *Evidence-Based Practice: A Critical Appraisal.* Oxford: Blackwell. pp. 212–241.

Watts, A.G. (2014). Career development: looking back; moving forward. iCeGS 17th Annual Lecture. Derby: International Centre for Guidance Studies. Available at: www.derby.ac.uk/media/derbyacuk/contentassets/documents/ehs/icegs/Career-development.pdf [Accessed 9 June, 2016].

Useful resources

Below are some publications that will help you explore more about research and evidence-based practice.

Blaxter, L., Hughes, C., and Tight, M. (2010). *How to Research.* (4th edn). Buckingham: Open University Press.

Bowes, L., Hartas, D., Hughes, D., and Popham, I. (2003). *A Little Book of Evaluation.* Derby: University of Derby. Available at: www.proveandimprove.org/documents/LBE.PDF [Accessed 9 June, 2016].

Bryman, A. (2004). *Social Research Methods.* Oxford: Oxford University Press.

Higher Education Funding Council for England (HEFCE). (2014). *Higher Education Outreach to Widen Participation: Toolkits for Practitioners. Toolkit 4: Evaluation.*
(3rd ed). Bristol: HEFCE.

Tristram Hooley's blog, Adventures in Career Development: https://adventuresincareerdevelopment.wordpress.com

Hughes, D. and Gration, G. (2009). *Evidence and Impact: Careers and guidance-related interventions.* Reading: CfBT. Available at: www2.warwick.ac.uk/fac/soc/ier/ngrf/effectiveguidance/improvingpractice/curriculum/cfbt_ei_online_resource_2009.pdf [Accessed 9 June, 2016].

Machi, L. and McEvoy, B. (2012). *The Literature Review: Six Steps to Success.* Thousand Oakes: Corwin.

Oliver, P. (2010). *Understanding the Research Process.* London: Sage.

Silverman, D. (2011). *Interpreting Qualitative Data.* (4th edn). London: Sage.

Reflection page

6 | CPD for self-employed practitioners

Introduction

Many people working in the career development sector are self-employed. Some work as career coaches or career consultants, others as talent managers. In recent years, an increasing number of career advisers who were once employees have become self-employed, working either as sole traders in schools or as part of a small company.

Both of us are qualified career advisers and at different times in our careers have been self-employed. We found this type of work exciting, rewarding and challenging. It increased our appreciation of the many transferable skills which career advisers possess and how self-reliant and resourceful we needed to be to keep our existing skills and knowledge up to date as well as developing new skills that being self-employed demanded.

The purpose of this chapter is to look at how people who are self-employed can undertake CPD. What are the challenges and barriers, and how can these be overcome? How can you future-proof yourself and perhaps diversify into other areas where you can use your skills and knowledge? What is the value of looking at CPD for your whole career and not just your immediate needs?

This chapter is about:

- the challenges to undertaking CPD
- determining your CPD needs
- knowing what you can offer
- acquiring more strings to your bow
- accessing CPD opportunities
- return on investment
- networking
- using a mentor
- using your skills and knowledge in other contexts
- international CPD
- future-proofing yourself.

The challenges of CPD

There are various challenges to undertaking CPD when you are freelance.

- How do you decide on what you need, and then how do you access it?
- As a self-employed practitioner your money and your time are your own, so how do you ensure a return on your investment in terms of value for time and money?
- The network of colleagues that you had when you were employed may not be as easily accessible once you are freelance. So, what do you do to keep in touch with people who can provide professional support and potential work opportunities?
- How do you maintain your confidence in what you are able to do?

Determining your CPD needs

Keeping up to date with changes in legislation and technology is as important to a self-employed practitioner as it is to someone who is employed. What is different when you are self-employed is that it is up to you to be alert to what the changes are and to then source information about them. This is where undertaking a Political, Economic, Social and Technological (PEST) analysis as part of your own CPD programme can prove very useful.

Activity

	What will the change be?	How will this impact your work?	What do you need to do?
Political			
Economic			
Social			
Technological			

Being a member of a professional body that provides members with regular updates about sector developments can help to alert you to changes and can even suggest ways in which you can update your knowledge. Professional networking can also help in this regard, as can the use of relevant government or assembly websites.

- England: www.gov.uk
- Scotland: www.scottish.parliament.uk
- Wales: http://gov.wales/?skip=1&lang=en or http://gov.wales/?skip=1&lang=cy
- Northern Ireland: www.niassembly.gov.uk

Keeping your existing skills and knowledge up to date and developing these is equally important. Determining what CPD you need as a self-employed practitioner is done in the same way as if you were employed; see Chapter 2. To this, you may also need to add keeping up to date with developments in your clients' organisations by looking at relevant websites, meeting new colleagues or following relevant blogs; learning more specialist skills and knowledge and looking at ways you can advocate for your profession and your new role within it.

Some freelance roles may also require specific qualifications and you may need to consider formal CPD and undertake some award-bearing qualifications. For example, where project management is involved in your freelance work some potential employers require PRINCE2 qualifications.

Knowing what you can offer

Looking at the verbs in National Occupational Standards: Career Development titles can show you what skills and knowledge you already have. Albeit in a career development context, these skills can also be used elsewhere beyond the career development sector.

- **Develop and apply understanding of theory** and effective practice in career development.
- **Reflect on, develop and maintain own skills and practice** in career development.
- **Build and maintain relationships with individuals** to ensure a client-centred approach to career development.
- **Support individuals to identify and explore** their career development needs and aspirations.
- **Enable individuals to set appropriate goals** and career development objectives.
- **Plan and deliver individual and group development** through career-related learning.
- **Enable individuals to use and apply information** for career development.
- **Provide ongoing support to help individuals** achieve their career goals and development objectives.
- **Help individuals evaluate their progress and achievement and plan for the future.**

- **Lead and manage** career development work in an organisation.
- **Improve services to individuals by collaborating with others.**
- **Enable individuals to access referral opportunities.**
- **Represent individuals' needs to others.**
- **Plan and design the service offer.**
- **Promote the availability, value and effectiveness of the service.**
- **Monitor, evaluate and improve the effectiveness of the service.**
- **Plan and undertake research on behalf of the service.**

By looking at the NOS: CD in detail you can see what other skills and knowledge you have that can be transferred to other working contexts as well as being used in self-employed career development practice.

Reflection

Skill/knowledge you already have	Where this skill/ knowledge is demonstrated in your current work?	Where or how else could you use this skill/ knowledge?	What aspect of the skill/knowledge would you need to develop further to use it in a new context or as a self-employed career development practitioner?

As well as being a useful CPD activity, the above can also act as a confidence booster and be useful as a checklist when completing bids and tenders for new work.

Acquiring more strings to your bow

When you are self-employed you wear many different hats, some of which will fit you well as you already know what to do, while others will be uncomfortable at first as you develop the necessary skills and knowledge to fit your needs. You may be comfortable as a career development practitioner but once self-employed you may also be: manager; accountant; administrator; negotiator; marketeer; IT support; Health and Safety support; and, if you employ staff, a HR person too. Some of these skills you may already have, others you may need to develop or you may decide which areas of your freelance work you are prepared to pay for someone else to do. Developing these different skills can be really interesting and add to your confidence as well as adding further strings to your freelance bow.

Reflection

Self-employed role, e.g. accountant, IT support, marketeer, etc.	What I do well already and how this can be improved	What I need to learn and how I will do this

One of the ways in which you can look at what skills and knowledge you need to develop for some of the non-career development roles is by looking at the relevant National Occupational Standards for that particular sector. Use the National Occupational Standards Database to search for relevant NOS and use the performance criteria as a checklist for your further development. For example, the NOS on 'Plan how to let your clients know about your products or services' can provide you with a useful list of things that you would need to know and do. Some of these you could work out for yourself, but for others you may want to look for a course you could attend or resources that you could access via the internet or through a relevant professional body, e.g. Chartered Institute of Marketing.

The British Chambers of Commerce (BCC) is also a useful source of information and can provide information on setting up a business as well as access to business services, policy and news and a range of events: www.britishchambers.org.uk.

Why undertake CPD when you are self-employed?

In Chapter 2 we looked at why CPD is important and the motivations for undertaking it. Similar reasons exist for undertaking CPD when you are self-employed, but to these can be added the ability to give yourself a competitive edge, especially as it can demonstrate your resourcefulness and responsibility to your client and to your own work. Prospective clients will also want to see your commitment to up-to-date practice and adherence to a code of ethics.

Membership of a relevant professional body and professional registration can also be valuable when tendering for work, and registration depends on undertaking CPD. However, once registered you can use your professional status when tendering for work, as well as being able to use professional logos on your stationery, website, etc.

Accessing CPD

If you were an employee before you became self-employed then you will have been used to having CPD activities provided for you. As a freelance worker you need to develop your resourcefulness and to look on this as a valuable personal skill that you can use to market yourself. Being able to demonstrate to a client that you have the ability to not only determine your own CPD needs but to also find imaginative ways in which to meet them, can provide you with a further competitive edge.

The A to Z of CPD in Chapter 9 can provide you with lots of useful ideas, and the case studies at the end of this chapter show you some examples from real life.

The websites of professional bodies and other organisations are also a useful source of CPD activities. Here are a few examples:

- The Career Development Institute (CDI) website has a CPD Resources section for its members, providing access to information about online learning, published resources and live training events. These are all categorised under the 17 National Occupational Standards: Career Development so that members can use these NOS: CD if they wish to analyse their CPD needs and then find relevant activities.
- The CIPD (professional body for HR and people development) website also has a resources section containing survey reports, factsheets, policy reports, guides, research reports, podcasts, practical tools, employment law FAQs, legal timetables and more.
- The Association of Graduate Careers Advisory Services (AGCAS) has a resources section containing reports, DVDs, web and print resources.
- Websites of trade associations, such as Careers England, are also a source of useful information, especially their policy commentaries which are independently commissioned analyses of key policy areas relating to government plans and policies.
- Sites such as ACAS are useful for finding out about employment legislation and the policies you may need to have for your own business. When tendering for work you often need to include your Equal Opportunities policy, etc. and the sites below are a mine of helpful information.
    - England: www.acas.org.uk/index.aspx?articleid=1461
    - Scotland: www.acas.org.uk/index.aspx?articleid=1949
    - Wales: www.acas.org.uk/index.aspx?articleid=1950
    - Northern Ireland: www.acas.org.uk/index.aspx?articleid=1461

Using social media as a source of CPD is a topic in its own right, and further information about this can be found in Chapter 7. Social media can also help to raise your professional profile, and this is a valuable thing to do when you are self-employed. You could add this to your CPD plans if you need to know how to set up your own website or how to use LinkedIn to raise your professional profile.

Return on investment

Working out the return on your investment can follow the same cycle you would use when determining your CPD needs and then undertaking the activity: assess your needs; identify the appropriate CPD activities for those needs; plan those activities into your schedule, including the time to practise what you have learned; carry out the learning; record the activities you have undertaken; evaluate their worth to you; reflect on what you have learned, what you will do differently, and what additional CPD you might need; implement the knowledge in practice; continue to review, reflect and revise and assess your needs again.

However, to this you may also like to add working out what additional charges you may be able to make for your services given that you will have a new skill or knowledge. For example, if undertaking a course in psychometric testing costing a certain amount means that you can now offer this service at a certain price to your clients and you are likely to have a certain number of clients requiring this, then does having undertaken this training make financial sense?

Time is also money, so if an activity is going to take you so many hours/days to complete then calculating how much this will cost you in terms of 'lost' earnings is a useful calculation to make. You then need to weigh this against how much more money you will be able to earn as a result of your newly developed skill or understanding.

Travel costs of training events also need to be added to the equation. Is it more cost effective to attend a conference where there are lots of learning and networking opportunities as opposed to a single-subject event? Is it more cost effective for you to learn online and network virtually than spend money travelling to venues?

Some training costs may be tax deductible. As the law on this may change, we have not given details here but suggest that you contact your financial adviser or HM Revenue and Customs for the latest information: www.gov.uk/government/organisations/hm-revenue-customs.

Networking

When you work for yourself you can find the whole experience very liberating: there is no boss to tell you what to do and you can, up to a point, decide on your own working hours and holidays. There are downsides, too: no sick pay or holiday pay, no certainty of income and no colleagues back at the office from whom to seek support. You need to develop the mindset of being able to fend for yourself but also to know from whom you can seek support when you need it. This is where networking as part of your CPD can be useful, as you can use it to seek support from others in the network, learn new skills or develop existing ones and, in some instances, find out about future work opportunities.

Networks can be real or virtual. The latter are becoming increasingly popular and can save time and money spent on travelling to attend real-life meetings. Knowing which virtual networks to access for different aspects of your CPD is useful; for example, for asking and answering questions, virtual networks such as LinkedIn, Twitter, Quora or Yahoo Answers can be useful, provided that you use your critical faculties to judge the answers you receive. To receive feedback on your work, you could try YouTube, SlideShare or Vimeo. For specific areas of your work you may like to use Communities of Interest, such as those offered by the CDI in specific areas: www.thecdi.net/Communities-of-Interest. Here you can pose and answer questions, seek and share new knowledge or information, ask for advice, share ideas or concerns, etc.

You can also set up your own networks, either real or virtual, and use these in a similar way. As a career development practitioner you will already have many of the skills needed to network successfully and you may already have people from your employed life with whom you can network.

Networking is also a useful way of developing personal skills as well as your professional ones. As part of your CPD planning you may like to look at which of your personal skills you need to develop further; for example, self-confidence; resilience; creativity; curiosity; reinvention; coping with change; problem solving; ability to talk to people you do not know; flexibility on how you can use your own skills and knowledge; doing something that is out of your comfort zone; resourcefulness; negotiation skills; advocating for the value of what you can offer, etc.

From personal experience, we know that being self-employed can sometimes be a lonely existence unless you make the effort to network, and this energy has to come from you. Having a set of reasons why you should network both virtually and in person can be a useful motivator. Here are a few examples.

- **Sharing knowledge:** this is great for your own CPD. You can ask for feedback on your work, find out what others think and gain insights on the perspectives of other people. They may know of other sources of information and be able to recommend further CPD opportunities. Having a CPD activity recommended can save you time in sourcing it and can also mean that you can find out more about its benefits before you commit yourself to the time and money needed to undertake it. In a network, you also need to be prepared to give as well as take, so sharing your own knowledge is a vital part of this process.
- **Seizing opportunities:** this may be a referral or request for your service or product. It is important to be ready to seize opportunities when they come along. Having an open mind to how you can use your existing skills and knowledge and being open to using these in different ways can lead to a range of new business opportunities. If this then leads to you needing to learn new skills and knowledge then these are further strings to add to your freelance bow.
- **Making connections:** each person in your real or virtual network will know other people. By networking with them you gain exposure to these people too. If someone they know has a need that matches your business you may get a referral.
- **Trading CPD opportunities:** as some CPD activities can be expensive it is worth seeing if anyone in your network is willing to share their skills and knowledge with you in return for you doing the same. For example, someone may provide you with a basic session on how to use Excel for your accounts in return for you providing them with some tips on job interview techniques or how to make their CV more effective.
- **Increasing your confidence:** growing your business relies on you being able to talk to people and make connections. Regular networking helps to develop this self-confidence and ability to talk to people whom you don't know.
- **Raising your profile:** sharing your knowledge and skills and providing support to your fellow network members will earn you a valuable reputation. By regularly attending real and virtual networks, people will begin to recognise you and think of you when work opportunities arise.

Some people who are self-employed can find sharing knowledge within a network difficult, especially if this knowledge is commercially sensitive and hours of blood, sweat and occasional tears have gone into its development. Our advice is that this needs to be a personal judgement. Thinking through what you will receive in return for your sharing of knowledge and what benefits this may have to you can sometimes mean that sharing your knowledge is worthwhile. Most people will respect the fact that certain knowledge is commercially sensitive and either will not ask for this to be shared or if they do and you do not wish to share it they will then respect your view.

Reflection

Who is in your network?	Are they a source of support/new learning/new work opportunities?	What do you provide to them?

Activity

How could your network be improved?

____

____

How will you do this?

____

____

Setting up a professional network and raising your professional profile

In a 2015 article in *Career Matters*, Charles Handy provides some useful insights into using LinkedIn to raise your professional profile and to develop your own network. He suggests that Identity, Network and Knowledge are the core ingredients for success. He says that Identity is about you in a work/career context and, importantly, about who you want to be in the future. Networking, he suggests, is not just about networking for today but also for the future. In relation to Knowledge, Handy recommends LinkedIn as a great source of knowledge on career paths, employers, jobs and industries.

Google+ is also gaining in traction. In another 2015 article in *Career Matters*, Ruth Winden shares her top ten benefits for using Google+, including as a means to teach, share and learn through Google+ hangouts. She recommends their free online video conferencing tool as a webinar platform or learning/teaching tool. This can be a useful source of CPD for you as a self-employed practitioner, but Google+ can also help you to create an online presence; engage with more people; find Communities of Interest and people with common interests; save money (as it is free to use); have real conversations; benefit from an array of tools; use your creativity to build a substantial profile and stand out when you engage with potential employers/clients.

Using a mentor

Having a mentor can also provide a means of professional support. Someone with whom to sound out your ideas and from whom you can learn. Your mentor can provide you with advice and encouragement; help you to solve problems for yourself; encourage you to reflect on your practice and help you to improve your self-confidence. As a self-employed person, you may like to look at having a business mentor who can help you to develop those skills above and beyond the career development skills you will need to run a successful business.

As well as helping you to improve your skills and knowledge, a mentor can also be a person with whom you can let off steam. Articulating what makes you cross or what you find difficult about your role to another person can often be the first step in helping you to decide what steps you can take to overcome your frustrations. As a result of these conversations, planning what CPD to undertake to overcome your difficulties can be a healthier activity than reaching for the wine bottle.

Mentors themselves can also be a useful source of business contacts. They may be able to put you in touch with other people who can help you to learn new professional skills or recommend people who can help you with your accounts or designing your website.

Although some mentor–mentee relationships are short-term, if you get on well with your mentor, you can foster a long-lasting relationship through which you and your mentor can continue to collaborate for the rest of your career. This will provide you with the continuity and resources you need to maintain a successful business. Mentors can also be a great source of confidence when you have to make difficult business decisions. Praise from a mentor can provide a real confidence boost. Seeing yourself as an experienced self-employed practitioner can be beneficial and give you the impetus to stand your ground when negotiating contracts or making difficult decisions.

We know from our own experiences of being self-employed that starting a business can be difficult and many people face challenges early in the process. However, many self-employed people go through the same types of struggles. Hearing first-hand from your mentor about their experiences will help you realise that the struggles you are going through now are nothing new and will prepare you to be a stronger professional in the future.

Being a mentor yourself can also be a great source of CPD and you may find that many of the interpersonal skills you already have as a career development practitioner will equip you well for this role. You may be able to offer this as a charged service or you may find that the benefits in terms of your own professional development are sufficient reward. Being a mentor can give you the opportunity to reflect on own practice; enhance your role satisfaction; help you to develop professional relationships; enhance recognition from your peers; provide the satisfaction of making your experience available to another person; widen your knowledge of the sector and the way it works; and enhance your own self confidence in your professional skills and knowledge. You may also learn new ideas and methods from your mentee and make new contacts that will enhance your own professional network.

Using your skills and knowledge in other contexts

Putting all of your freelance eggs into the one basket is ill-advised, especially if the basket relies on short-term government funding. One of the skills of being self-employed is keeping an eye on where opportunities for further work can present themselves, and this should be an ongoing part of your work. Some work may not necessarily be in areas in which you directly use your actual career development skills, but may apply those skills in other ways. For example, one of us used her knowledge of how to write qualifications for the career development sector and applied this to writing qualifications for the youth justice sector and HM Prison Service. Utilising interview and research skills developed as a career adviser she was able to find out what youth justice and Prison Service roles involved and then write appropriate qualifications and training programmes. Her CPD for that piece of work covered: learning about the roles in the different sectors; finding out how to write qualifications that can be offered in higher education and how to have these accredited; gaining the confidence to present the qualifications to academics and senior civil servants; and improving, what were, at the time, her very basic IT skills.

Although an initially scary experience, branching out into a different field but with the reassurance of a solid and relevant skills and knowledge base and the willingness to learn new information, meant that this diversification was a positive experience and a very useful source of CPD.

CPD as a daily activity

Being self-employed means that you are no longer part of the annual staff development/appraisal cycle which may have been used to determine your CPD needs in the past. In fact, when you are self-employed you may find that your need for CPD can be very much an ongoing process and that you need to learn specific things for particular pieces of work very quickly.

Being exposed to different ways of working also means that your opportunities to treat every day as a training day are increased. You can find that you are a sponge to new ideas, skills and knowledge. Often you can transfer these to different aspects of your work. Finding the time each day to reflect on what your day's experience has taught you and to note down these new ideas, ways in which you might use them and also what the day has taught you about any gaps in your knowledge and what further CPD you need is time well spent and can enrich your self-employed experience. Chapter 4 on reflecting on practice will provide you with insights on the different ways to do this.

International CPD

As already mentioned, the body of knowledge for the career development sector in the UK has drawn upon theories from other disciplines, for example, sociology, psychology and education. It has also learned lessons from how career development services are provided in other nations. As a self-employed practitioner you may have the opportunity to deliver papers at international conferences or visit career development services abroad. These are very useful CPD activities and much can be learned and shared from these.

However, the use of the internet means that the world has shrunk, and many insights into international working can be sourced online. The CPD skill of reflection on what you have learned and how this can be transferred to different situations means that you can use a variant of this skill to read about international perspectives and then ask if these would work in your context, if they could be adapted and whether this would result in better outcomes for your clients.

Activity

Look at the following websites and ask yourself what you can learn from the way in which career development services are offered in other countries.

Careers New Zealand:
www.careers.govt.nz/practitioners/career-practice/research

International Centre for Guidance Studies (iCeGS):
www.derby.ac.uk/research/icegs/publications

Scan the list for those relating to other nations and see what you can learn that can inform your own practice.

Future-proofing yourself

As an employed or self-employed career development practitioner, being aware of developments in the sector and how your skills and knowledge need to develop to keep pace with these developments is key to your successful and continued employment. Rather than only thinking of your CPD needs in terms of the immediate future, it is beneficial to also think in the medium and longer terms too so that you do not miss out on future work opportunities simply because your skills and knowledge are out of date.

If you reflect back on how much the career development sector has changed in the last decade you can see how those people who did not embrace the increased use of technology were left behind. Similarly, those people who thought that they had a job for life may now find it difficult to adapt their skill sets to working for themselves or within a different context. Although crystal ball gazing is not an exact science, it does pay to keep an eye on the way in which the sector is developing and to factor this into your CPD planning.

One way of doing this is to use a Strengths, Weaknesses, Opportunities, Threats (SWOT) analysis and to marry this to a PEST analysis. How the career development sector will evolve over the next five or ten years can also be a useful discussion point for real or virtual networks, and from this you can add the points of view of others to your own analyses.

Conclusion

In this chapter we have looked at the value of CPD when you are self-employed and the different means that you can use to develop your professional self for both your current role and any roles you may perform in the future. From our own experiences we would say that being self-employed is a continuous state of professional development, and that by being open and alert to all professional development opportunities presented to you, you are able to maintain and grow your business.

To conclude with a musical analogy, as a self-employed practitioner you may feel that you are a solo player playing a particular instrument. But by adding further strings to your bow, practising and reflecting on what you can do, and with the accompaniment of your network and with your mentor providing some musical direction, you can continue to play a happy tune of your own composition for many years.

Case Study: Bev Ashby: Director - Bev Ashby Associates

Background

My career has spanned many years in Human Resource Management working as HR Director at Board level. I qualified with the Chartered Institute of Personnel and Development (CIPD) and gained a Master's in Business Administration and undertook a number of other development programmes. From a very early stage in my career I have always been interested in what makes people 'tick' and why they respond in the way they do to different situations, hence why human resource management has been the right career path for me.

My own personal career journey changed in 2013 when I decided to set up my own executive coaching and mentoring business. I had always wanted to do this as it felt a natural progression following a full-time career in Human Resource Management, where I had coached and mentored many people at all levels in the organisation. I wanted to work with people who were facing challenges in their career, and the impact this was having on both their work and home life. I knew I had a lot of experience in a large organisation guiding people through their career journey, and felt that this was an area of specialism I wanted to delve into further.

However, being self-employed requires a different mindset. You have to drive the business and obtain clients – they don't just walk through the door. You need to ask yourself a number of questions: what is my passion, what is my purpose and do I have the necessary skills and experience that people want?

As the world of coaching is largely unregulated, I wondered how my client would know they are working with an appropriately qualified experienced coach. I therefore wanted to explore this further before setting up my own business. I asked myself the question, 'would I use my services?' The answer was yes, but I would want to know more about my credentials and qualifications and why they should work with me.

I knew that my skills were pretty good given my experience as an HR Director, but I didn't have the formal coaching qualification and for me that was pretty important.

While I was developing my own business and undertaking the coaching qualification, I decided to write to the local high schools to offer my help coaching and mentoring sixth-form students on a voluntary basis. I have been working with one school for two years and it is probably the best thing I have done in my career. Young people need all the help and support they can get to prepare them for the world or work or university. I work with groups and individuals across a wide range of practical issues, including CV writing, work experience and mock interview practice.

The skills and knowledge I needed

There were a number of things I needed to do. The first were regarding my own competence: did I feel I had all the necessary skills and knowledge to work as a self-employed practitioner? I also needed to understand the mechanics and practicalities of setting up my own business. I wanted to stand in front of potential clients with the knowledge that a coaching qualification gave me authenticity, which is so important for me. A number of colleagues challenged me as to why I was doing the qualification, saying all the right things: 'It's a natural skill you have', 'I know you would always help me find a solution', but these were people that already knew me. My new clients wouldn't have this knowledge about me. I also learned so much about myself as a coach, as part of the programme was being coached yourself. The ILM Level 7 Postgraduate Certificate in Executive Coaching and Mentoring was the right programme for me.

I did the programme via a local company; it had a really good balance of theory and practice and the time for coach practice. The other benefit was working with like-minded people with the same common purpose; many who were looking to work independently. It was well worth the time and money and I felt very proud when I gained the qualification; I had done this for me.

The great thing about being self-employed is you get to work with so many different organisations and clients. However, you cannot afford to stop learning and developing your practice. I am constantly looking for new theories and practice to ensure I remain up to date and authentic for every client. I read widely and belong to a number of networks and have regular supervision sessions to ensure I am working at my best. Having undertaken the Alternative Qualifications Route to the register I am also a CDI Registered Career Development Professional.

Top 5 tips for CPD for the self-employed

1. Build a good network with like-minded people with whom you are able to share ideas and, most importantly, gain knowledge and experience from. Being self-employed can be lonely at first so having people to call on is really essential.
2. Many clients are introduced based on your reputation, so make sure you continue to develop and learn so that you are up to date and have new ideas to offer clients. It's no good talking

about old theories and practice if these have been replaced with different thinking; it will undermine your credibility.
3. Keep up to date with professional memberships; they provide great access to the latest information and research.
4. Always research in advance the company or client you are going to meet; you will learn a lot and understand the context in which they work. This is all good CPD.
5. Never stop learning, when you do it may be time to pack up what you are doing!

My own CPD

1. Take time out for personal professional development. I consider it essential to spend time doing this. This can be networking events, seminars, meeting with like-minded colleagues to share ideas or issues. I do this through peer and individual supervision.
2. Use social media. I am an avid user of LinkedIn, and have joined a number of groups. People will post articles that you can read at any time. It's easy to access.
3. Ask for feedback from every client. This enables me to continuously improve my practice. I keep a notebook of reflections; it is always good to reread and challenge yourself.

Examples of some of the networking groups I belong to and materials I read on a regular basis are:

1. LinkedIn, as the various networks I belong to post articles that provide lots of information about career development/transition etc. This is really easy, as you can do this at any time.
2. HR Review – this is an online daily article that I subscribe to.
3. CIPD journals and local West Yorkshire networking group. I also belong to a local CIPD self-employed group.
4. I am a member of the European Mentoring and Coaching Council and the Association for Coaching and join their webinars on a variety of topics that you can use in coaching.
5. I follow 'notgoingtouni' on Twitter and online, which is really good for keeping up to date with changes.
6. I am a member of Coaching York networking group.
7. I am a member of the International Society for Coaching Psychology, which is another LinkedIn group.

Apart from these local and online groups, I am an avid reader of a wide range of texts to continually improve my practice. A recent book is *Your First 100 Days: How to make maximum impact in your new leadership role* by Niamh O'Keeffe, which is really helpful for people who are changing roles or being promoted.

Case Study: Liz Reece: Career Development Consultant

In addition to the careers education and career guidance and networking skills that I developed while employed for 27 years, when self-employed I found I needed to develop skills and knowledge in finance, administration, marketing and promotion, and how to contract with clients.

I also keep my professional skills up to date by deciding which CDI or other career development courses to attend within a budget (since training incurs travel costs and time away from paid work), being resourceful and motivated to read, research and update skills.

Most of my learning in how to set up my business was self-directed, some involved a little discussion with others, and some was based on the retail management training that I did as my first graduate job. I also visited a business adviser; while he was very interested in my business plan, he simply endorsed all that I was doing and suggested that I set up different websites for the variety of career development work that I offer.

The skills I have developed are used most days in some way or another as they are part of running a business. I have not attended any specific courses for the skills that I have developed in self-employment, although a CDI workshop for career advisers on contracting with schools has been very useful background to developing contracts.

Top five tips for the self-employed

1. Service: think about the level of service that you expect from other services and try to provide this to your clients.
2. Diversify: expect work to be diverse; you might need to extend how you apply your career education and guidance knowledge by using different skills, e.g. in research or writing.
3. Network: don't be afraid to ask for guidance from other self-employed colleagues and if you really don't feel confident about taking on a piece of work, pass it on. You are likely to find this favour comes back later!
4. Finance: keep it simple and organised, and save all your receipts.
5. Keep cool: there are manic times and quiet times and part of the art of success is to cope with both while constantly looking for the next job. You might need support from your partner and family when things are particularly stressful – communicate this to them.

Examples of some of the activities I do for CPD are:

1. Reading a wide range of media: articles in books and magazines, and on the internet through Twitter and LinkedIn.
2. Reading the CDI News via Email newsletter and following up many of the links given to update myself.
3. Downloading and reading all the PowerPoints made available by the CDI, even if I haven't been able to attend the training; this has proved fantastic CPD.
4. Being an associate at iCeGS and attending meetings when I can and learning from these and reading articles on the website.
5. Attending some training events when taking students on trips.
6. Talking to colleagues and following up new points.
7. Researching on behalf of clients, which ensures that I am up to date on things such as university undergraduate or postgraduate admissions.
8. Meeting with Career Mark colleagues, which ensures that we maintain understanding of developments around the country as well as in quality standards.
9. Undertaking Career Mark assessments: I learn from each one!
10. Paying to attend training if I have weighed up the likely costs and benefits, e.g. those run by CDI, UCAS, local authority.

Case Study: Dave Cordle: Career Coach

I had changed career to become a Career Coach and, although I was good at this, I believe in a more holistic approach and, indeed, I often found that my clients too had other areas of their life that they wished to work on and would benefit from doing so.

I had already joined ACP International (one of the founding organisations of the CDI), and started a rigorous accreditation process with ICCI (the Institute of Career Certification International). The combination of potential extra benefit to clients and certification helped me to really think about how to best approach the subject of CPD given that, being self-employed, I needed to maximise the value I got from any CPD activity.

The CPD activities below are some of the main CPD activities I have undertaken during my Career Coaching career and represent those that made the key differences. I have read many books, conversed with many coaches and other professionals, attended many conferences and smaller training events, all of which keep me up to date with the latest thinking in the industry and in personal development. They help me to grow and develop personally and as a coach, and to help my clients produce even better results for themselves.

Certificate and Diploma in Life Coaching: This gave me more skills and coaching strategies to work with people in areas other than careers and also helped me become a more effective Career Coach. For example, this was where I first came across the GROW model of coaching. I chose this particular course from the thousands out there because it was sponsored by a recognised educational establishment and sponsored by the Learning and Skills Council.

Solution-focused Brief Therapy: I'd heard about this through my network and took this mainly because I was fascinated by this approach to coaching and I thought it might have some use in career coaching. I found it more useful than I imagined and still use some of the techniques from the toolkit today.

NLP Practitioner and Master Practitioner: Both these courses were a major investment of time and money, but have given me skills that I use every day in career/business coaching and which have helped me to personally be the best coach I can. I have used these particular skills and techniques as major inputs to services that I provide to create transformational results for clients; for example, helping people to change their beliefs about what it is possible for them to achieve.

Top five tips for CPD for the self-employed

1. Do it regularly and do it often.
2. Look for things you enjoy, as these will help you grow personally as well as in business.
3. Keep up with what's going on so that you can pick relevant training to help you do your job better.
4. Review your training regularly so that you get the most from it. Practise if you can, and always ask for help if you need to.
5. Think about whether you'll get a return on the investment, be it directly, indirectly or in the long term – and remember that return isn't always just financial.

Examples of some of the activities I do for CPD are:

1. Major training as above.
2. Workshops/conferences where I get to network with other professionals in similar and different industries. Often the conversations I have are as valuable as the actual training.

It also helps me to build relationships with people where we can perhaps work together in the future (I'm always looking for win/win/win opportunities).

3. Reading books and listening to audio (e.g. TED talks). A lot of coaching knowledge has been around for decades (sometimes centuries), and my practice is enriched by learning new things and by viewing things I perhaps already know from new angles and perspectives.
4. Practice groups (especially NLP) which allow me to practise techniques I don't use often, and play with techniques that I do use in different ways, thus helping me use what I know in ever more effective ways.

References

Handy, C. (2015). Giving yourself the best chance of success. *Career Matters,* October, pp.22–23.

Winden, R. (2015). Google+: the social media powerhouse that deserves your attention. *Career Matters*, June, pp.8–9.

Useful resources

Below are a number of websites that may be useful in helping to access help and support as a self-employed practitioner.

Association of Graduate Careers Advisory Services (AGCAS): www.agcas.org.uk

British Chambers of Commerce (BCC): www.britishchambers.org.uk

Career Development Institute (CDI): www.thecdi.net

Careers England: www.careersengland.org.uk

Chartered Institute of Personnel and Development (CIPD): www.cipd.co.uk

Federation of Small Business: www.fsb.org.uk

National Occupational Standards Database: http://nos.ukces.org.uk/Pages/Search.aspx

Reflection page

7 | The internet, social media and international CPD opportunities

Introduction

Over the last two decades, careers work has changed immeasurably as a result of technology. This has resulted in changes in how we access and use careers information, labour market information (LMI), apply for jobs and interact with our clients. More recently, social media in particular has had a significant impact for all of us both professionally and personally – whether you love it or loathe it, you can't ignore it.

In this chapter we will examine:

- how social media has influenced our professional practice
- the importance of being digitally literate within the world of career development
- social media tools that can support CPD
- being passive and proactive in terms of our CPD
- international opportunities to engage in CPD.

We have already made the point that it is difficult to function as a career development practitioner if you are not able to use IT. This is also an issue for clients, but actually many of them are social media savvy and are often keen to utilise email/Facebook/text in their relationships with career development practitioners. We want to focus on how *you* can use and maximise the opportunities that social media offers for your own CPD. In addition, we want to explore some more creative ways of engaging in CPD, such as being a 'CPD tourist' and using social media to build an international network and to engage with CPD opportunities in other countries.

The internet, social media and career

We all agree that the world we work and live in is influenced almost daily by changes in technology. Whether it is through accessing new software, apps or websites, our lives are changing incrementally through technological developments. When many of us started as careers advisers the main source of occupational information was *Occupations!* If you don't know what this was, it was the bible of careers, and contained LMI on all the major occupational areas.

Once upon a time, young people could only get to university via Clearing through their local careers service as the careers advisers had access to information about available places. All of this has changed dramatically, and careers work, as with all other professions, has been inundated by technological changes.

> *It is not sustainable to continue to view the internet solely as a tool which can aid (or challenge) the careers worker: rather there is a need to see the internet as an integral part of the social fabric and to recognise that it provides a major context in which career development is enacted.*
>
> *(Hooley, 2012: 3)*

All of this you know! So, in this chapter we want to focus on how you can develop your career using social media.

But what is social media?

> *Social media are computer-mediated tools that allow people or companies to create, share, or exchange information, career interests, ideas, and pictures/videos in virtual communities and networks.*
>
> *(Wikipedia, https://en.wikipedia.org/wiki/Social_media)*

So basically, social media is a way of sharing with other people online. It might be with people you know and people you don't know. Increasingly, it is about maximising the capability of mobile technology as more people have access to smartphones. These are phones that incorporate features of a computer with a mobile phone. This technology allows you to connect with people almost instantly. Many people will also have access to a tablet; again this is a wireless personal computer with a touchscreen.

Common tools used on the internet

Facebook is an online social networking site: www.facebook.com

Google is a search engine and advertising website: www.google.co.uk

LinkedIn is an online professional networking site: www.linkedin.com

Prezi is a cloud-based presentation software: https://prezi.com

SlideShare is an online tool to share PowerPoint presentations: www.slideshare.net

WordPress is a site that provides facilities for blogging: https://wordpress.com/create

Twitter is an online microblogging and social networking site; the Twitter hashtag # is a way for people to search for tweets that have a common theme: www.twitter.com

But thinking about yourself for a moment, how has your CPD been influenced as a result of technology and social media?

Activity

Just for five minutes think about the CPD you have engaged in over the last five years – how has technology and social media changed your experience over this time?

____

____

____

____

____

____

Digital career literacy

To be effective in using social media for CPD and to develop your career, you need to be digitally literate. This is described by Hooley as '*the ability to use the online environment, to search, to make contacts, to get questions answered and to build a positive professional reputation*' (2012: 5). Although Hooley is referring here to your role in working with your clients, it is equally applicable to ourselves as practitioners.

To be effective as a career practitioner we need to be supporting our clients to use social media to:

- access careers and labour market information
- transact with employers and learning providers
- develop networks and build contacts
- communicate with others who may have similar interests and concerns.

(Hooley, 2012)

It is worth thinking about how digitally literate you are in your own career. Ask yourself the following questions. Score each of these questions using a number from 1 to 5; 1= daily, 2= a couple of times a week, 3= every couple of weeks, 4 = occasionally, 5 = never.

1. How often do you search for information online to develop yourself and your career?
2. How often do you transact with employers and learning providers online for yourself?
3. How frequently do you engage with online networks and increase your list of contacts?
4. How often do you engage with others online to discuss your similar interests and concerns?
5. How often do you use social media to promote your online presence?
6. How often do you check your online presence (self-googling or ego surfing)?

What do your answers tell you about yourself and how engaged you are with developing yourself using social media?

The internet and social media are dynamic, which means that the way that you use them in your CPD is likely to change over time. There are new tools and websites coming along every day; some last for years and become fully integrated in our lives and consciousness, such as Google and Facebook, other such as Friends Reunited have a shelf life and get superseded. The important point about all of this is that there are new sites coming along all the time and it is useful to have a sense of these and which are going to be most useful to you. But be careful not to chase all new technology; you need to be selective and try out what you think might be useful to you. It is also a good idea to share what you learn with others so that you can learn collectively.

There are some good places to start when using social media for your CPD. For example, you might want to register with LinkedIn, Twitter and Facebook (although the latter is more often used as a social tool). One thing that you might want to do is separate out work and personal accounts. Do you really want photos of you fooling about at a friends' wedding being accessed by all those in your professional network?

Facebook

Facebook was founded in 2004. It has a mission 'to give people the power to share and make the world more open and connected'. It has become one of the most successful online tools and has over 1.59 billion users! Many people use Facebook for keeping in touch with friends and family, for sharing what is happening in their life at the moment and sharing pictures. Facebook is also increasingly being used for more commercial activities – my hairdresser keeps in contact with her customers by Facebook!

Within a careers context, Facebook is developing a wider use. Many National Careers Service providers have Facebook pages and encourage their customers to follow them. Advisers communicate and keep in contact with their customers through Facebook as well. It can also be a useful way of building social groups that have a common interest either between colleagues or professionals working across a wider area.

As with all social media, consideration needs to be given to how we present ourselves online. It requires individuals to take responsibility for what they write and the profile that they present. There are lots of stories of employers checking interview candidates out online. Think about what your Facebook account says about you if you are using it more widely than with just your immediate friends.

Getting started

If you do not know where to start with any of these tools, below are some weblinks that will help you to get up and running using basic social media tools.

Twitter: https://support.twitter.com/articles/215585

Using hashtags '#': https://support.twitter.com/articles/49309

Facebook: www.youtube.com/watch?v=KR_xVgt9iZk

LinkedIn: www.careerealism.com/getting-started-on-linkedin-quick-guide/

YouTube: www.youtube.com/watch?v=Hsuy4cUJe9o

Once you have registered your accounts, make sure you give yourself some time to build your network: start promoting your Twitter name in your correspondence with colleagues, and search for groups on Facebook and LinkedIn that are interesting and fit in with areas you may want to develop professionally. Once you are connected, start a discussion thread on an area of interest. There are lots of LinkedIn groups that focus on career issues.

Careers-related LinkedIn groups

Here are just a few of the groups that might be of interest to you. Some are open, which means anyone can join, others are closed, which means you need to apply to become a member.

The CDI has a number of LinkedIn groups and Communities of Interest you can join, including:

- Higher education advisers
- Independent coaches and consultants
- Careers education
- Career development research
- Learning difficulties and disabilities
- Student career practitioners.

Other groups you might be interested in:

- Career Thought Leaders
- Careers Advisers
- Careers Debate
- Career Professionals Network
- Association of Career Professionals International
- Careers Service Professionals
- ICT in Careers Work.

There are also groups focused on occupational areas and employers.

Building your online profile

Once you have set yourself up with lots of online accounts, the next step is to build your online profile so that people know who you are and what you are about. Having a profile and keeping it up to date is important so that you have visibility on the internet and people can find you and connect with you quickly. This is your personal brand and it is important that you have control over it: it is what you want people to know about you and what you want to promote about yourself. This is particularly important if you are looking for a new job, becoming self-employed or setting up your own business. In the next section we will provide you with lots of examples of activities that can help you to build an online profile.

Social media tools

There is a wide range of social media tools that you can use to support your continuous professional development. In this section we introduce you to the key ones; there are others. Remember this is always going to be a snapshot in time. Generally, social media tools can be divided into three main types: communication, collaboration and multimedia usage online. Figure 7.1 below (adapted from Beckingham 2011) provides a brief overview of some of the main resources that you may be familiar with.

Communication

Social media has changed how we communicate with each other. From a CPD perspective it is incredibly useful as it provides us with a way of communicating between ourselves but also, as individuals, to communicate with many people, a large number of which we have never physically met nor indeed are likely to. You can use many social media tools for CPD and for building your online profile.

- **Blogging.** A blog is a regularly updated website run by an individual or group of people and written in a conversational style. There are lots of different types of blogging or weblogging as it is also known. It has become very popular in recent years and provides a useful source of information. It is basically an online journal where the author will 'post' an entry. Bloggers encourage people to 'follow' them and to comment on their blogs, contributing to an online discussion. Sites such as WordPress provide webspace for individuals to create their own blogs. Blogs

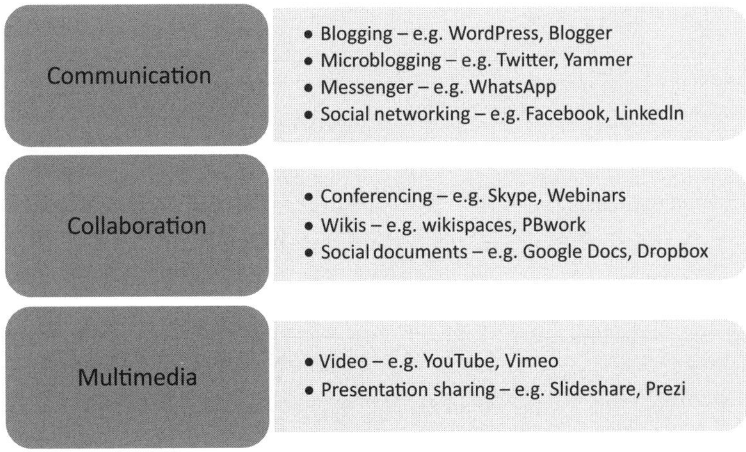

Figure 7.1: Social multimedia tools

can be thematic, focusing on a particular subject area (see Tristram Hooley's blog, 'Adventures in Career Development', https://adventuresincareerdevelopment.wordpress.com), or they can be generic where someone blogs about whatever they are interested in at that point in time. Other careers-related blogs you might be interested in following include:
  - https://secondaryceiag.wordpress.com
  - https://runninginaforest.wordpress.com.

  If you start to follow one, you will quickly find other blogs that may be of interest to you.
- **Microblogging.** This is most commonly **Twitter**, and has a slightly different function. Here people post short messages. This is useful for CPD as people share information they have found that they think will be useful and interesting to people following them; they may post information on jobs and opportunities, conferences, presentations they are giving or are attending. One of us, for example, tweets on careers, university, women's issues and anything related to work.
- **Messenger.** There are lots of facilities to send texts from your mobile phone and increasingly through computers. For example, WhatsApp is a tool that facilitates group messaging and can be used to send images and audio messages. Again, this tool can be used to update people on new information. In one of our offices we use it for sharing news items that will be interesting to colleagues.
- **Social networking.** These are the tools that most people will be familiar with and include Facebook and LinkedIn. Both of these facilitate access to registered friends, family and colleagues. LinkedIn is specifically focused at business and professions to help build online networks. Both of these can be used to informally assess people as part of a recruitment process. All are excellent ways of building your online profile, as well as developing discussions and sharing information for professional as well as personal purposes.

There are a number of useful publications that can help you to build your online profile and to use social media effectively to communicate with others on a professional basis. Have a look at *Building Online Employability: A Guide for Academic Departments* by Longridge, Hooley and Staunton (2013) and *You're Hired! Job Hunting Online: The Complete Guide* by Hooley, Bright and Winter (2016).

Collaboration

It is often difficult to find the time to meet up and work with others. There is a range of social media tools that can help you to connect, collaborate and work with others without having to leave your office or home.

- **Conferencing.** We are increasingly trying to find ways of reducing the cost, time and environmental impact of travel. There are many new ways to maximise contact with people without having to travel long distances. Within the realms of CPD, Skype and webinars (seminars that take place over the internet) have become ways of engaging in one-to-one and one-to-many discussions. The CDI uses webinars as a way of providing access to CPD that is accessible and free to members, whereas one of the professional associations for careers practitioners in Canada runs an annual virtual conference to support the professional development of its members.
- **Wikis.** A wiki is a website that allows collaborative modification of content. The most well-known is Wikipedia, where multiple authors can contribute to a single article. Developing wikis on particular topics is a good way of sharing knowledge and workload if you are developing materials or resources.
- **Social documents.** Often we need to share resources or materials we are working on, e.g. a conference presentation or an article. These tools are a useful way for groups of people to comment on, review or contribute to a document. They allow a number of people to work on a document at the same time so everyone can contribute and see the amendments. Google docs is a useful way of doing this; all participants will need to have a Google account.

Multimedia

Social media has opened lots of opportunities for us to learn from each other using interactive and video-based technology. These are easily accessible and useful when delivering training sessions.

- **Video.** There are lots of opportunities to use video to support your CPD. This can be through building your knowledge via sites such as YouTube, or even creating your own videos and posting them online for colleagues, and can be a really good way of sharing learning.
- **Presentation sharing.** There are a number of websites that you can use for this, such as SlideShare. A benefit of this approach is that you will always have your presentations in one place, and uploading your presentations is a good way of contributing to others' CPD. If you want to develop your skills in this area, Prezi is an interesting way to deliver presentations and a lot more creative than using PowerPoint all the time!

Social media and conferences

Even while you are engaging in CPD activities social media is central to the proceedings. While most conference/training/seminar sessions still use PowerPoint, video or Prezi to deliver the content, how you hear about these events may well have changed in recent years. How are you hearing about the conference/training? Is it through word of mouth, email, or have you found out about it from your LinkedIn groups or your Facebook contacts, or did you see a tweet on Twitter advertising the event?

The use of technology doesn't stop when you get to the conference. Inevitably, people will be on their phones and computers and some of them will even be talking about the conference! For example, they might be using Twitter to communicate with other people at the conference or with people who aren't there. One way to do this is to use a Twitter #hashtag. A Twitter hashtag is how Twitter groups tweets together, e.g. people who are communicating online about a conference might tag all of their communications on Twitter with #careersconference.

Posting messages about an event that you are attending is an interesting way of sharing highlights and points of interest with people who are not attending the event. It also provides people who are attending the event with a back channel where they can discuss what is being said by conference presenters while the presentations are going on.

All of these technologies can provide you with better access to information as well as connecting you to like-minded people across the world.

Other online CPD tools and resources

In the previous section we looked at social media resources that can be used to share and provide access to learning and knowledge to enhance professional development. There are many online tools and resources that can be used; some of them will be formal learning activities and others may be informal. Have a look in Chapter 9, the A–Z of CPD, and see some of the tools and resources that you can use to support your CPD using social media and the internet. There is an increasing amount of online learning opportunities that are available. Have a look at Massive Open Online Courses, commonly known as MOOCs, and OpenLearn in particular as these offer a wide range of courses that you can do online and for free, and they are easily accessible. You can build them into your work life quite easily. Many of the courses have been developed so that they can be used with smartphones, tablets, etc.

Again, it is important that you identify how you will use what you learn and find ways to share your learning.

Do make sure you research the potential usefulness of materials or resources that have costs attached before you commit and part with your hard-earned cash!

Passive and proactive CPD

Throughout the book we have provided a discourse around why CPD is important from a wide range of perspectives: professionalism, developing practice, building the profession, etc. One of the issues around CPD raised by Mulvey (2004) is that CPD can just be counting the hours. What Mulvey means is that you can engage in CPD activities but if you don't use or do anything with it then this is a huge cost to all with little return on investment for yourself and your employer if you have one.

When engaging in CPD we think there is a continuum. At the one end there are what we term **passive consumers** and at the other there are **proactive creators**. Much of the time many people may see themselves in the middle, which is fine. What we would want is for people to be aware of the different roles they may take in relation to their CPD: sometimes they may have a more passive engagement, and other times they may want to have a more creative and active role – not just consuming or engaging, but creating CPD for themselves and their colleagues.

We see these categories as particularly pertinent when exploring CPD using social media, although they do not just apply within this medium. It is important to state that there is nothing fundamentally wrong with either of these states, as each of them is an important mechanism for engaging with CPD activities. What we would say is that practitioners need to mix it up and sometimes be a passive consumer and other times be a proactive creator, as by engaging in both you will learn more. Let's have a look at what each of these looks like in practice.

Passive consumer

When we talk about being a 'passive consumer' of CPD what we are referring to is that individuals are passively experiencing CPD. This means they may be participating in CPD activities but may not be maximising the opportunity in thinking about how they may use the learning. This is not necessarily a negative as we are always learning, both consciously and subconsciously, however it is important that we reflect on what we have learned.

On the following page are examples of being a passive consumer.

- Being on a LinkedIn group where you read the responses and follow the discussion threads but you don't contribute.
- Being on mailing lists for organisational newsletters which you read.
- Watching TED talks on topics that are of interest to you: www.ted.com.
- Having a Twitter/Facebook account where you regularly check the messages.
- Following people on Twitter or relevant and interesting blogs.
- Reading an article that is relevant to your practice.
- Attending a conference or training session.
- Engaging in a webinar.
- Joining a professional association or body.

Activity

Which of the activities in the list above do you currently engage in?

____

____

____

Identify three new ones that could help you to develop your practice and how you would use these.

____

____

____

Also, think about how you might engage more actively in some of these activities.

1. ______________________________

____

2. ______________________________

____

3. ______________________________

____

TED Talks

Below are a few TED Talks we liked.

'How to find work you love' by Scott Dinsmore
www.ted.com/talks/scott_dinsmore_how_to_find_work_you_love?language=en

'The careers advice you probably didn't get' by Susan Colantuono
www.ted.com/talks/susan_colantuono_the_career_advice_you_probably_didn't_get#t-47555

'Your body language shapes who you are' by Amy Cuddy
www.ted.com/talks/amy_cuddy_your_body_language_shapes_who_you_are

'A kinder, gentler philosophy of success' by Alain de Botton
www.ted.com/talks/alain_de_botton_a_kinder_gentler_philosophy_of_success

'How to make choosing easier' by Sheena lyengar
www.ted.com/talks/sheena_iyengar_choosing_what_to_choose

Proactive creator

Proactive creators are those who actively contribute to CPD either through responding to other people, undertaking activities or sharing their learning. They will take a role in contributing to developing the evidence base and knowledge for the profession.

Below are examples of how you can be a proactive creator of CPD.

- Establish a Community of Interest group on LinkedIn.
- Tweet ideas, thoughts or articles that you find interesting.
- Establish a Facebook group for an area of interest to share ideas.
- Write a blog and promote it to your colleagues.
- Write an article for a professional publication or journal.
- Respond to requests for help with research and contribute your thoughts.
- Submit a workshop/paper for conferences and symposia.
- Seek to be elected for a professional body.
- Volunteer to act as an online mentor for less experienced colleagues.

- Post comments on blogs about topic areas/contribute to the discussion.
- Post comments on newspaper articles discussing your topic area.
- Deliver a webinar to your colleagues or for a professional association.

Activity

Which of the activities in the above list do you currently engage in?

____

____

____

Identify three new ones that could help you to develop your practice and how you would use these.

1. ______________________________
2. ______________________________
3. ______________________________

However, as mentioned, being proactive is not necessarily always a positive stance to take. If you are always leading then you may not have the time to learn from others or reflect on what you have learned. The ideal is a combination of activities; in some you will be a recipient and in others you will be proactive. Participating in social discussions about your CPD is not necessarily about leading networks, but engaging with others is an important part of learning and reflecting. It is important that we have a wide range of people promoting their views and contributing to the development of professional practice. If you are new or inexperienced in the profession, it may be that you feel more comfortable being a passive recipient. As you gain in confidence and develop your own expertise you should seek to be more proactive.

Within the sector, we need to develop and recognise advanced practitioners. These are the people who are developing expertise and extending professional practice. As an advanced practitioner, you should be leading the field and contributing to professionalising the sector.

Being a CPD tourist

One of the really inspiring elements of the internet is that engaging in CPD can happen at any time and anywhere in the world. Wherever you are based, there are opportunities to learn from others. One thing that is always either encouraging or disappointing, we are not sure which, is that when you talk to career development colleagues in other countries they often have similar issues linked to resources, demands of clients, policy and targets! There are a number of ways that you can engage in CPD with colleagues overseas and the next section explores a number of ideas that you might want to consider.

International activities

There are a wide range of international conferences and symposia that focus on career issues every year. It is great to have a paper or workshop accepted to present, and to share your knowledge with colleagues from across the world. This is an excellent form of CPD, both in terms of learning and in building an international network. Examples are:

- International Association for Educational and Vocational Guidance (IAEVG): http://iaevg.net/ – it has an annual conference which alternates between European and worldwide destinations.
- Euroguidance – The European Association of Career Guidance is a network that links lifelong guidance and international mobility across Europe. They offer an annual conference and events in different European cities focusing on career-related topics. http://euroguidance.eu/events-2.

Professional bodies and associations

There are a large number of professional careers associations across the world for the career sector.

The Institute of Career Certification International (ICCI) is an independent international body which establishes competencies and standards for professionalism within career management. It provides industry events and resources. Its main focus is to provide accreditation for career management practitioners. Information about the ICCI can be found at www.careercertification.org.

Many international organisations have annual conferences providing opportunities for practitioners across the sector to get together. Some of these conferences are vast international affairs, such as that of the

National Career Development Association (NCDA) in the US: www.ncda.org/aws/NCDA/pt/sp/home_page. The NCDA organises a conference every year in the US which attracts a lot of participants. Although there are cheaper rates for members, non-members are welcome to attend. It also operates the resources repository Vocopher: www.vocopher.com, which provides access to materials from Mark Savickas, Donald Super and other authors that may be of interest to some practitioners. More information about this can be found in Chapter 9, A–Z of CPD.

Many of the professional associations also produce regular newsletters and online e-zines. These are often openly accessible and offer interesting insights into some of the issues and practices in a particular country. Below are a few that you might want to explore. There are obviously many more than these, but we have focused on English-speaking countries for ease of access.

In **Canada**, CERIC (Canadian Education and Research Institute for Counselling) hosts an annual conference – Cannexus, http://ceric.ca. CERIC also has a weekly newsletter that anyone can sign up to and contribute articles to.

There are a number of professional associations in **Australia**. The largest is the Career Development Association of Australia (CDAA), which hosts an annual conference: www.cdaa.org.au. The CDAA provides access to interesting and useful resources on their website.

In **New Zealand** there is the Career Development Association (CDANZ), www.cdanz.org.nz, whose e-zine is accessible and has useful and interesting articles of interest to many career practitioners wherever they are based.

The **Republic of Ireland** has the National Centre for Guidance in Education (NCGE), www.ncge.ie, which produces an excellent newsletter (NCGE news) focusing on issues for guidance counsellors in schools as well as those who work with adults.

Attending international conferences is an expensive activity in terms of both registration and travel. It may be worth considering linking a holiday to a conference you have always wanted to attend.

We have also known many colleagues who have used the opportunity of a long-distance holiday to investigate the local careers provision. A colleague going on holiday to India built in a day to meet with one of the career guidance organisations. They ended up presenting to their hosts about their careers work in the UK. This provided a really interesting opportunity to learn more and to build their international network.

Even if you are not able to attend any of these conferences in person, copies of the papers and the workshop presentations will be available on the conference website. It is worth finding a conference you would be interested in and attend virtually by downloading the presentations and materials. You can also engage at a distance through looking for Twitter hashtags and associated webinars. Often, for example at iCeGS, the annual lecture is recorded so those who cannot attend can still view the lecture.

Activity

Set up a wish list of international conferences you might like to attend.

What is it about these conferences that you feel would benefit your practice?

How else might you meet this need?

Erasmus+

Other useful opportunities for international CPD are European projects. Erasmus+ is the programme that coordinates the funding for a wide range of European opportunities focusing on study, work, training, teaching and volunteering in activities related to lifelong learning across Europe.

These include:

- mobility projects for learners and staff in HE and vocational education and training (VET)

- mobility projects for staff in school education and adult education
- Erasmus Mundus Joint Master's Degrees
- Erasmus+ Master's loans
- strategic partnerships
- knowledge alliances
- sector skills alliances
- capacity building in the field of higher education.

A mobility project focuses on setting up a partnership activity, implementing it and evaluating it within the field of education and training. This can be a good way of sharing an innovative activity that you may have been involved with.

Strategic partnerships aim to support the transfer and exchange of innovative practice.

Although the funding for engaging in these activities can be complex, Erasmus+ does offer a useful way to build European and international networks. Information about the various opportunities can be found at www.erasmusplus.org.uk/what-can-i-do. Please note, European funding may not be fully available in the future as a result of Britain's decision in June 2016 to leave the EU, however a limited number of non-EU partners have been able to join projects in the past.

In this section we have focused on ways of engaging with colleagues outside of your daily contacts and considered ways in which you can broaden your network and access knowledge and learning from colleagues working in other countries. There are lots of opportunities to think creatively about what you can do to enhance your existing network.

Conclusion

Final thoughts: if you are interested in exploring more about digital literacy and how it supports careers work, have a look at Hooley (2012) listed in the reference section below. Reid's (2016) book has a chapter on using digital technology for careers work; this is useful for thinking about blending career development activities with technology.

There are lots of new and exciting ways to engage in CPD! It is not all about attending training courses. In the modern world CPD should not be restricted to where you can get to. Career development practitioners are busy people and need to access and engage in CPD in ways that mirror and reflect the other types of activities in their lives. Being able to access bite-size learning through tablets and smartphones provides useful ways to build CPD into daily activities.

References

Beckingham, S. (2011). Social Media and CPD? You can't be serious. ... Available at: www.slideshare.net/suebeckingham/social-media-and-cpd [Accessed 9 June, 2016].

Hooley, T. (2012). How the internet changed career: framing the relationship between career development and online technologies. *Journal of the National Institute for Career Education and Counselling*, 29, pp.3–12.

Hooley, T., Bright, J. and Winter, D. (2016). *You're Hired! Job Hunting Online: The Complete Guide*. Bath: Trotman.

Longridge, D., Hooley, T. and Staunton, T. (2013). *Building Online Employability: A Guide for Academic Departments*. Derby: International Centre for Guidance Studies.

Mulvey, R. (2004). Can I stop now? The role of continuing professional development in professional practice. In: H. Reid and J. Bimrose (eds), *Constructing the Future: Reflection on Practice*. Stourbridge, Institute of Career Guidance.

Reid, H. (2016). *Introduction to Career Counselling and Coaching.* London: Sage.

Useful resources

A few more tools and resources for consideration.

White, J. (2015). *Digital Literacy Skills for FE Teachers*. London: Sage.

Tristram Hooley's blog, Adventures in Career Development: https://adventuresincareerdevelopment.wordpress.com/tag/socialmedia

Sue Beckingham's blog, Social Media for Learning: https://socialmediaforlearning.com

'What is a Blog?': www.youtube.com/watch?v–jwUHXoi8lM

Reflection page

8 | National Occupational Standards and competence frameworks

Introduction

Globalisation and modernisation are creating an increasingly diverse and interconnected world. As the career development sector is constantly evolving, it is vital that you have the means to demonstrate that your professional skills and knowledge are fit for purpose. Many of the requisite skills and knowledge you will have learned as part of your initial training for the role you perform, but – as we have said frequently throughout this book – there is also the need to update these and to do this as part of your own continuous professional development. If you are intending to move or have already moved into a careers teaching or leadership role or into a self-employed role, you will need to develop skills and knowledge relating to your new role as well as maintaining and developing those required for your original role.

Having a standardised and credible way to review these skills and knowledge is important. In this chapter we will look at various standards and frameworks which can help you to do this and suggest ways in which you can use them.

As well as looking at the National Occupational Standards used in the UK, this chapter will also look at competence frameworks that are used across Europe and elsewhere in the world. It is useful to see what competences are needed internationally, and to see the similarities and differences that exist between your own country and those required elsewhere.

There are many competence frameworks for career development in use and space here does not allow us to cover them all. We have selected a number of different types to explore and activities to help you consider them within the context of your own practice development.

This chapter is about:

- why we have competence frameworks
- what is competence?
- National Occupational Standards
- NICE competences
- Framework for qualifications and CPD for the career development workforce in Scotland
- Scottish Subject Benchmark Statement for Career Guidance
- Institute of Career Certification International (ICCI) competencies.

Why do we have competence frameworks?

Sultana (2009) says that competence (or competency) frameworks are generally developed for two reasons. The first is to identify competences in ways that enable the assessment of performance in relation to set standards. The intention here is mainly to manage staff, or to establish levels of competence attained after initial, induction or in-service training. A second motive for developing frameworks is to provide a guide for self-evaluation and self-development, as well as for training programme development.

This paper is well worth a read for what it says about some of the debates surrounding the term 'competence' and the relevance that these have for the development of competence frameworks.

What is competence?

There are various definitions and the above mentioned paper by Sultana explores some of them. In the Cedefop report 'Professionalising career guidance: practitioner competences and qualification routes in Europe' (2009), the following definitions are provided.

- Cognitive competence, involving the use of theory and concepts, as well as informal tacit knowledge gained experientially.
- Functional competence (skills or know-how), involving those things that a person should be able to do when they are functioning in a given area of work, learning or social activity.
- Personal competence, involving knowing how to conduct oneself in a specific situation.
- Ethical competence, involving the possession of certain personal and professional values.

For the career development sector, we think that these are useful definitions as they include the use of knowledge that is gained experientially and also emphasise the need for ethical competence as well as functional and personal competence.

The rest of this report is also worth looking at as it presents the findings from a Europe-wide study that addressed two purposes, namely to:

- review trends and patterns in training provision for career guidance practitioners
- develop a common competence framework for career guidance practitioners in the European Union.

Sections 5 to 7 of the report focus on the competence framework of career guidance practitioners. These sections explore the concept of competence, the design of the competence framework and suggestions for its use. Section 8 explores ways of moving forward, and links the two strands of the project by relating current and proposed training issues to proposed uses of the competence framework.

What is also interesting to see when reading this report is how much the world has moved on. It presents a number of international and national frameworks that have been developed through various international collaborations, transnational projects and national initiatives. Some of these are still of relevance today, but others that have been produced more recently could now be added, such as the National Occupational Standards for Career Development (NOS: CD) or the NICE Core Competences.

In some countries the development of competence frameworks has only recently begun. The Competency Framework for Career Development Practitioners in South Africa, produced by the Department of Higher Education and Training in 2015, draws on a number of existing frameworks and provides a very useful summary of them, including the transnational frameworks from IAEVG, Cedefop and NICE and national frameworks from the USA, Canada, Republic of Ireland, Australia, UK and Scotland.

What is clear from the development of these competence frameworks across the world is that they do not stand still. Just as the career development profession is evolving, so are the competence frameworks. What is also striking is that although there are many similarities between all of the frameworks that help to give career development an international identity, there are also differences that relate to the particular national contexts in which services are delivered. When using these frameworks for your own CPD purposes it is vital that you source up-to-date ones that are relevant to your own context. However, looking at ones from other nations is also interesting and can provide you with ideas about how you might diversify your practice.

National Occupational Standards (United Kingdom)

National Occupational Standards (NOS) (CDI, 2015a) are statements of the skills, knowledge and understanding needed for effective performance in a job role, and represent a consensus view and description of best practice for each particular function, having been developed and agreed with a range of employers and stakeholders representing the sector area.

They can be regarded as the benchmark of competence required in the sector and form the key component of many qualifications. They apply to and are used across each of the four UK nations, are developed using a UK-wide approach and are approved by agencies acting on behalf of the relevant government departments in each nation of the UK.

NOS are produced as a suite of standards for each occupational area. Each standard comprises a number of performance criteria that an individual should demonstrate to be competent in. Each standard also outlines the knowledge and understanding that underpin the standard.

NOS are designed as a resource for individuals and organisations to use to improve their capacity and capability, and can be used to help define job roles, measure staff performance and identify and develop routes for progression and professional development.

As an employed or self-employed career development professional or as a manager of practitioners, you can use the National Occupational Standards: Career Development (NOS: CD) for you or your staff to:

- develop self-confidence and enhance effectiveness
- provide a means of determining gaps in knowledge, experience and skills
- offer an objective process for determining training needs
- support professional development
- open up a wide range of career opportunities
- help to transfer skills and knowledge to other situations
- demonstrate competence when tendering for freelance work.

NOS are also an excellent but often under-utilised source of careers information, so you can use the NOS for other sectors as part of your role with clients. Looking at the NOS Database will show you just how many NOS there are and how useful they can be when explaining what various job roles involve.

NOS can also be used in a variety of ways by:

- employers for organisation and workforce development
- education and training providers for assessment and benchmarking, and development and review of learning programmes

- professions and professional bodies for regulation of qualifications and institutions, identification of skill gaps and requirements for training provision, public recognition of competence, production and endorsement of resources, courses and events, and in the case of the CDI (which is the custodian of these NOS) as the basis for the Career Progression Pathway and the Alternative Qualifications and Competency Routes to the UK Register of Career Development Professionals.

Further information on how NOS can be used by employers can be found in the Resource Guide for Employers on the CDI website (CDI, 2015b).

There are 17 National Occupational Standards for Career Development.

1. Develop and apply understanding of theory and effective practice in career development.
2. Reflect on, develop and maintain own skills and practice in career development.
3. Build and maintain relationships with individuals to ensure a client-centred approach to career development.
4. Support individuals to identify and explore their career development needs and aspirations.
5. Enable individuals to set appropriate goals and career development objectives.
6. Deliver individual and group development through career-related learning.
7. Enable individuals to use and apply information for career development.
8. Provide ongoing support to help individuals achieve their career goals and development objectives.
9. Help individuals evaluate their progress and achievement and plan for the future.
10. Lead and manage career development work in an organisation.
11. Improve services to individuals by collaborating with others.
12. Enable individuals to access referral opportunities.
13. Represent individuals' needs to others.
14. Plan and design the service offer.
15. Promote the availability, value and effectiveness of the service offer.
16. Monitor, evaluate and improve the effectiveness of the service offer.
17. Plan and undertake research on behalf of the service.

Each job role throughout the career development sector will require a number of these NOS, but you will be pleased to learn that no one role will require all 17!

To see which NOS are of relevance to particular levels of role in the different parts of the sector, take a look at the Career Development Sector Progression Pathway on the CDI website: www.thecdi.net/Career-Development-Sector-Progression-Pathway. The pathway shows the different branches of the sector: Career Education; Career Guidance/Development and Career Coaching/Talent Management. It also shows the roles within them: First Contact; Support; Practitioner; Specialist Practitioner; Manager; Senior Manager; Research/Technical and Specialist Role: Lecturer; Consultancy; Inspectorate. It covers the qualification levels required/recommended and where career mobility is possible. As some of the roles are management ones, there is also reference to the NOS for Leadership and Management.

To give you some ideas on how the NOS: CD can be used to help with your own CPD you may like to undertake the following activity.

Activity

Look at your job description and determine which of the 17 NOS are relevant.

Select one to concentrate upon, and then follow the example in the box below.

For example, if you provide career guidance you may like to look at: *Develop and apply understanding of theory and effective practice in career development.*

If you have a career leadership role you could consider: *Lead and manage career development work in an organisation.*

If you are self-employed you may like to look at: *Plan and design the service offer.*

Example

Develop and apply understanding of theory and effective practice in career development.

You will see that the NOS is divided into various sections. Firstly, there is the overview, which can help you to see if this NOS is relevant to you; it also provides information on topics that should be considered in relation to this NOS.

'Overview: This standard is about developing your knowledge base of theories, concepts, techniques, models of effective practice and contextual information – and using them to improve your own role and practice.

The topics about which you develop and apply your understanding could include self-awareness, aspiration raising, opportunity awareness, motivation, confidence-building, empowerment, networking, transition and change management, decision-making and avoidance, action-planning, option evaluation and identifying and accessing opportunities. They may also be related to career development practice, vocational behaviour or career management.'

Assuming that the overview is relevant to you, you can then move on to look at the performance criteria and knowledge and understanding and answer the questions.

Performance criteria. You must be able to:	How do you do this in your role? What evidence do you have?	How could you improve what you do? What action could you take to do this?
develop understanding of theories, concepts, models and techniques relevant to own role and area of expertise		
apply understanding of theory, concepts and effective practice in career development to own practice		
tailor and adapt models and techniques to own role and career development practice		
draw upon contextual knowledge resources, including relevant labour market intelligence, to inform career development practice		
keep own knowledge base and practice up to date		

continually review own practice based on developments in theory, concepts, models, techniques and approaches to effective practice		
share effective practice with other practitioners		

Knowledge and understanding. You need to know and understand:	How do you demonstrate this in your role? What evidence do you have?	How could you improve what you do? What action could you take to do this?
legal, organisational and policy requirements relevant to your role and the activities being carried out		
the range of topics you need to consider when developing and applying theory and effective practice in your role		
sources of relevant theories, concepts, models and techniques and how to access them		
sources of contextual information, including relevant local, regional, national and international labour market intelligence, and how to access them		
ways to evaluate theories, concepts, models, techniques and contextual information for their usefulness and applicability		

the contribution of evidence-based practice to the development of theories, models, concepts and techniques		
the purpose and application of research, reflection, self-evaluation and peer review in developing own practice		
the individuals, groups and networks you can work with to improve your own and others' understanding of theory and practice and how to build relationships with them		

The questions can form part of your CPD planning as part of your **self-awareness** of your needs. You can then start to look at **opportunities to meet your CPD needs**. Once you have **acted** and undertaken the CPD, you can use the above as a checklist again to **reflect and record** how the CPD has helped, where you have been able to use your developed skills/knowledge and to what effect, and to determine if you have further needs. As part of your CPD, you can then **share** what you have learned with your colleagues.

As this book is about Continuous Professional Development you may also like to try this activity based on the NOS 'Reflect on, develop and maintain own skills and practice in career development'.

Activity

For any of the following performance criteria consider:

- Why do you do this?
- How do you do this?
- Who do you involve?
- When do you do this?
- What could you do to improve this?

Performance criteria

- Review and evaluate own skills, knowledge and career development practice against current performance requirements.
- Identify trends and developments relevant to own skills, knowledge and career development practice.
- Identify and critically reflect on how own values, beliefs and attitudes influence own career development practice.
- Seek feedback to reflect on and evaluate own performance.
- Ensure own career development practice is inclusive and promotes equality and diversity.
- Address internal and external constraints that impact on own practice.
- Plan and access development opportunities needed to keep own knowledge, skills and practice up to date and enable own work to be carried out more effectively.
- Use records of own actions, development plans and progress to support and inform ongoing reflective practice.
- Apply new knowledge and skills to consolidate learning and improve own practice.
- Review the effectiveness of newly acquired knowledge and skills.
- Engage positively with opportunities for support and supervision.
- Share effective practice with other practitioners.

NICE Core Competences

The Network for Innovation in Career Guidance and Counselling in Europe (NICE) is an academic network of 45 higher education institutions in 29 European countries. In 2012 it published the *NICE Handbook for the Academic Training of Career Guidance and Counselling Professionals* (Schiersmann et al., 2012), which includes chapters on:

- NICE Professional Roles (NPR): a common understanding of the professional function and the central professional roles of career guidance and counselling professionals
- NICE Core Competences (NCC): a joint competence framework with a nucleus of core competences which career guidance and counselling professionals need to perform in their professional roles

- NICE Curriculum: a competence-based curriculum framework of learning outcomes relevant for the training of career guidance and counselling professionals, together with references to methods of teaching, learning and assessment
- NICE Tuning Framework: a common theoretical framework for the development of degree programmes in career guidance and counselling, including a common language for doing so.

In this chapter we will concentrate on the NICE Professional Roles and the NICE Core Competences and suggest how you might use these for analysing your CPD needs. However, the rest of the handbook is well worth a read and provides insights on career guidance and counselling training across Europe.

NICE Professional Roles

These roles are all of equal importance in practice. Career guidance and counselling professionals can switch between these roles in their work, sometimes combining them, sometimes focusing on particular roles while leaving others out completely.

- **Career information and assessment experts.** Helping individuals to assess their own strengths and connect them meaningfully to the labour market and the education system.
- **Career educators.** Using pedagogic approaches to develop individuals' career management skills.
- **Career counsellors.** Using counselling, coaching and advice work approaches to help individuals to understand their situation and to progress in the labour market and education system.
- **Programme and service managers.** Working with individuals and organisations to design and deliver career development programmes.
- **Social systems interveners and developers.** Using networking, consultancy and advocacy skills to develop organisations and systems and to help individuals to succeed within them.

The handbook provides a useful example of these roles in practice.

> *A client could come to a career guidance and counselling professional unhappy about her/his current working position. While counselling the client (i.e. acting as a Career Counsellor), the professional could also employ assessment instruments to help the client understand him/herself better (acting as a Career Information & Assessment Expert). Furthermore, part of the same contract could include teaching the client how to engage more effectively in job interviews. Here, the career guidance and counselling professional would be acting as a Career Educator. In*

asking the client to fill out evaluation forms on the effectiveness of the working relationship between each of the sessions, the professional would be acting as a Programme and Service Manager. If the professional organised a talk between the client and an employer in her/his network, the career guidance and counselling professional would be behaving as a Social Systems Intervener and Developer.

(Schiersmann et al., 2012)

Activity

- Think of an example from your recent work and write a short description of what you did.
- Reflect on which of the roles given in the above example you performed and which of the skills mentioned in the example above you used.
- Now look at the following NICE Core Competences for each of the roles and determine if you would deem yourself to be competent, based on your chosen example, or if any aspects of your practice require further development.
- You may like to share your chosen example and what you did with a colleague and gain their perspective on your actions.

NICE Core Competences (NCC)

NICE Core Competences have been derived through a detailed comparison of the NCC with other existing competence frameworks, a curricular analysis of existing degree programmes in Europe, an analysis of innovative trends in the field of career guidance and a discursive process through which many members of the network have contributed their expertise.

Career Educators are competent in:

- teaching people how to become aware of their strengths (interests, values, abilities, competences, talents, etc.); how to use systems and techniques of gathering information on available jobs, vocational and educational training; how to plan, manage, implement and review their career; and how to apply effectively for working or learning opportunities
- developing curricula for training programmes
- planning training sessions
- facilitating learning in different types of groups and communities
- providing people with support on improving their competences for lifelong learning.

Career Information and Assessment Experts are competent in:

- providing clients with information and assessment methods that support them in autonomously assessing how suitable particular educational and vocational opportunities are for them
- communicating educational, organisational, societal and political requirements and opportunities appropriately, taking into consideration the needs and capacity of clients, and reducing the complexity of information
- explaining the world of work, vocational and educational systems, as well as trends and developments in the labour markets and educational systems
- making use of information systems
- employing different assessment techniques for identifying the strengths, weaknesses, opportunities and risks of clients.

Career Counsellors are competent in:

- supporting clients in dealing with complex biographical issues related to life, work and identity
- supporting clients in identifying solutions and making decisions related to complex career issues (e.g. setting goals and priorities)
- employing ideographic and reflective approaches (e.g. solution-centred questioning, storytelling, reframing)
- working alongside their clients in developing and pursuing goals over long periods of time, mastering career transitions and dealing with uncertainty (if necessary)
- motivating clients and supporting them in identifying and activating resources, allowing them to pursue their life-projects as autonomously as possible.

Programme and Service Managers are competent in:

- managing projects and ongoing operations
- presenting evidence to secure the services that best meet clients' needs
- setting up contracts with clients (individuals or organisations)
- marketing/advertising career guidance and counselling services and organisations
- ensuring compliance with relevant regulation
- making organisational decisions on how to manage resources (including their own time) effectively and efficiently
- leading colleagues and cooperating with significant stakeholders
- managing important information and knowledge
- assessing and evaluating the quality of career guidance and counselling activities (processes and outcomes)
- developing capacity for handling change and organisational development.

Social Systems Interveners and Developers are competent in:

- making arrangements with stakeholders within systems
- approaching and intervening with existing networks and communities and building new ones
- consulting organisations in career-related questions of their stakeholder (e.g. recruitment, placement or personnel development of employees, career management competences of pupils)
- making referrals
- coordinating activities of different professionals
- collaborating with different professionals (e.g. career workers, social workers, educators, psychologists, rehabilitators, probation officers, etc.)
- advocating and negotiating on behalf of their clients in relevant contexts (e.g. work teams, families, formal proceedings)
- mediating conflicts between clients and their social environments.

Activity

Take any of the above competences and think through what you do about this in your own practice. For example,

Teaching people how to become aware of their strengths (interests, values, abilities, competences, talents, etc.), how to use systems and techniques of gathering information on available jobs, vocational and educational training, how to plan, manage, implement and review their career, and how to apply effectively for working or learning opportunities.

- Why do you do this?

____

____

- How do you do this?

____

____

- Who do you involve?

____

____

- When do you do this?

____

- What sources of information do you use to inform your practice?

____

____

- What could you do to improve this aspect of your work?

____

____

Activity

Select any of the competences above and imagine that you were speaking with a less experienced colleague who wanted to know sources of CPD activities to develop his/her skills in this area. Note down what you would suggest.

____

____

____

____

If you encouraged a colleague or colleagues to undertake the same activity for the other competences you could swap ideas and use this as a means of generating a list of opportunities for CPD.

Framework for qualifications and CPD for the career development workforce in Scotland

In 2012 the Scottish Government established a short-life working group to develop a framework for qualifications and Continuous

Professional Development for the career development workforce in Scotland. The aim was to:

- improve awareness of current development opportunities, qualifications, support materials and progression routes for the career development workforce
- support a better understanding of professional development gaps
- provide greater clarity on how career qualifications relate to wider professional development frameworks
- increase related practitioners' awareness of careers development opportunities and qualifications
- encourage more informed strategies of employers to develop their staff, having regard to everyone's needs.

Although this is not a competence framework, we have included this here as it provides a useful section on the typical job roles, work tasks, attributes, entry requirements and accredited and non-accredited CPD opportunities.

Activity

Select one of the sets of attributes that are relevant to your role. For example, the attributes listed for a Career Adviser are: Interest in people; Impartial; Objective; Non-judgemental; Empathy; Confidence; Maintain confidentiality; Committed to equality and diversity; Adaptable and responsive; Analytical and Critical reflection on own practice.

- For each of the attributes note down how you demonstrate these in your practice.
- What evidence do you have?
- You may like to reflect upon these notes with a colleague or ask someone to observe your interaction with a client to note how you demonstrate relevant attributes.

Scottish Subject Benchmark Statement for Career Guidance and Development (2014)

Subject benchmark statements describe the nature of study and the academic standards expected of graduates in specific subject areas, and in respect of particular qualifications. They provide a picture of what graduates in a particular subject might reasonably be expected to know, do and understand at the end of their programme of study.

They are also useful to use as a checklist to see how you have maintained and developed your knowledge and skills post qualification. In the case of this benchmark, it has also been mapped to the Learning Outcomes of the Qualification in Career Guidance/Development (QCG/D), which is the only qualification in the UK awarded by the CDI as the professional body for the career development sector.

Activity

Look at the 'CDI Qualification in Career Guidance and Development Handbook', in which these benchmarks and the relevant QCG/D Learning Outcomes appear. Select a relevant section and note down what you remember learning about this during your training and how your skills and knowledge have developed since.

____

____

Identify any gaps in your learning and source means to address these.

____

____

In the Subject Benchmark Statement it says that those undertaking a career guidance and development qualification must be able to demonstrate, through their knowledge, understanding, skills and abilities that they are committed to:

ethical practice:

- working ethically
- accepting opinions and beliefs that differ from their own
- challenging others in cases of unethical or oppressive behaviour

excellent professional practice:

- engaging with clients in an open, honest and impartial way
- empowering clients to take decisions that are right for them
- trying innovative techniques to engage individuals and groups in career-related activities
- widening clients' horizons
- helping clients to understand opportunity structures

- working within the boundaries of professional competence
- respecting confidentiality and always seeking permission in cases of referral
- making appropriate referral of clients to other sources of support and accepting the right of clients to request referral to another adviser
- engaging proactively and creatively with employers and other opportunity providers
- partnership working with other organisations to build trust, mutual understanding and effective working relationships that benefit clients

reflective practice and professional development:

- engaging in constructive professional dialogue
- exploring new or unfamiliar ideas and experiences
- being reflective and professional
- engaging in personal improvement and continuous professional development
- sharing both positive and negative experiences with others
- recognising, valuing and learning from the skills and expertise of colleagues in own and other agencies
- keeping up to date with and exploring the contribution that theory can make to practice
- keeping up to date with developments in public policy and their impact on practice.

Activity

Looking at these lists, consider the following.

- When was the last time you did any of the above?

  ____

  ____

- Why did you do this?

  ____

  ____

- What was the outcome?

  ____

  ____

- Are there ways in which you could improve your practice in this regard?

  ____

  ____

- How will you do this?

  ____

  ____

- Who can help you?

  ____

  ____

Institute of Career Certification International (ICCI) Competencies

According to its website, the ICCI has evolved since its founding in 1994 to reflect the focus of practitioners and clients today. Founded as The International Board for Career Management Certification, the certification body represented a desire for the then unregulated outplacement industry to assure organisational and individual clients that services were of high ethical and professional quality. As the career management profession has adapted to meet clients' needs, the ICCI has expanded its certification criteria through updating competences and ethical standards to assure that certified practitioners represent excellence and ethics in all aspects of their career development and management services.

It is important to note that this body provides certification for learning that has already occurred. It does this by providing a series of competences that individuals meet via a range of approved validation methods. As with the other competences shown in this chapter, the ICCI competencies are a useful checklist to see if your skills and knowledge for working in this part of the sector are relevant and up to date. The current 'Core Competencies' are given on the following page. These are being updated during 2016; please see the ICCI website for the most up-to-date version.

Activity

Look at the following competencies and write a case study that includes:

- statement of the situation
- background of the situation
- issues to be resolved
- procedures employed
- outcomes
- summary
- principles of practice demonstrated
- competences demonstrated.

If you were faced with the same situation again, would you do anything differently and why?

Core Competencies

- Actively and continuously participate in personal and professional development in the career management field in order to be knowledgeable about best practices.
- Strengthen the career management capability of an individual or an organization by assessing, exploring, challenging, advising, recommending alternatives and providing feedback on assumptions, attitudes, behaviours and perceptions.
- Possess a broad knowledge of theories and approaches to career management services and apply the appropriate approach to meet the unique needs of a client.
- Demonstrate awareness of diversity issues and modify style and approach accordingly with clients and colleagues from different social, ethnic, gender, sexual orientation, religious, cultural, generational backgrounds and physical and mental capabilities.
- Possess broad knowledge of career assessment tools and processes. Demonstrate the effective use of at least one to assess a client's capabilities, needs and limits to create a foundation for career planning and implementation.
- Analyse and assess client's working environment in the context of business, political, social and economic factors.
- Develop strategies for learning and development to improve client's performance and further long term goals.
- Understand how an organization's culture impacts career management and use this knowledge to help clients develop effective career strategies.

- Assess when to refer a client with special issues/needs, identify external resources and, when necessary, link the client to those resources.
- Clarify client goals and objectives and establish an agreement regarding how career services will meet them, including service parameters, logistics, fees, commitments and outcomes. Keep accurate records and report appropriately to clients.
- Enable individuals to enhance life balance and professional growth by guiding them to identify and select among options that take into consideration life stage and individual development.
- Enhance awareness of the value of professional career management services, increasing the public's ability to discriminate wisely in selecting qualified practitioners who reflect the highest standards of our profession's values and expertise.

What changes have there been since you qualified?

If it's been a while since you qualified, at whatever level, you may like to have a look at the more recent versions of your qualification and use this to see if there are any areas in which you need to develop your skills and knowledge. The 'Getting Qualified' section of the CDI website provides access to the Learning Outcomes for the Qualification in Career Guidance/Development and the work-based QCF qualifications at levels 4 and 6.

The CDI also intends to publish a 'Blueprint of Learning Outcomes for Professional Roles in the Career Development Sector' that will be used to inform all professional qualifications for the sector, and you will be able to use this to reflect upon your own skills and knowledge.

Conclusion

We hope that this chapter has shown you the wide range of competence frameworks, standards and benchmarks that exist for the career development sector. As well as these being used for the development of qualifications, they are also really useful for CPD. Effective CPD demonstrates your commitment to being a professional and evidences that you have taken responsibility for ensuring that, post qualification, you continue to have the knowledge and skills required to practise as an effective, reflective practitioner and to meet the challenges of the ever-changing career development sector. Using these frameworks to analyse your CPD needs is part of the self-assessment part of the CPD process. The next stage is finding CPD to meet your identified needs.

Undertaking a mix of CPD activities will enhance your professional practice and refresh and extend your skills and knowledge. An underpinning principle should be that you understand why you are participating in the activity and what you expect to get out of it, and how you will use it in your practice.

Whether you are employed or self-employed, or are adding an additional responsibility to your existing role, finding ways to meet your own CPD needs can often be up to you. Therefore, in the next chapter we provide some ideas on the different methods you can use to meet your needs.

References

Career Development Institute. (2015a). *National Occupational Standards: Career Development.* Stourbridge: CDI. Available at: www.thecdi.net/National-Occupational-Standards [Accessed 9 June, 2016].

Career Development Institute. (2015b). *Resource Guide for Employers. National Occupational Standards: Career Development.* Stourbridge: CDI. Available at http://www.thecdi.net/write/Register/BP310-National_Occupational_Standards-v7.pdf [Accessed 9 June 2016]. Cedefop. (2009).

Department of Higher Education and Training. (2015). *Competency Framework for Career Development Practitioners in South Africa.* Available at: www.dhet.gov.za/Gazette/Competency Framework for Career Development Practitioners in South Africa.pdf [Accessed 9 June, 2016].

European Centre for the Development of Vocational Training: Luxembourg: Office for Official Publications of the European Communities. *Professionalising Career Guidance: Practitioner Competences and Qualification Routes in Europe.* Available at: www.cedefop.europa.eu/en/publications-and-resources/publications/5193 [Accessed 9 June, 2016]. Institute of Career Certification International (ICCI): www.careercertification.org.

QAA. (2014). Scottish Subject Benchmark Statement: Career Guidance and Development. Available at: www.qaa.ac.uk/publications/information-and-guidance/publication?PubID=14 [Accessed 9 June, 2016].

Schiersmann, C., Ertelt, B-J., Katsarov, J., Mulvey, R., Reid, H., and Weber, P. (Eds). (2012). *NICE Handbook for the Academic Training of Career Guidance and Counselling Professionals.* Heidelberg: Heidelberg University. Available at: www.nice-network.eu/wp-content/uploads/2015/11/NICE_Handbook_full_version_online.pdf [Accessed 9 June, 2016].

Scottish Government. (2012). A Qualifications and Continuous Professional Development Framework for the Career Development Workforce in Scotland. Available at: www.gov.scot/Publications/2012/07/5300 [Accessed 9 June, 2016].

Sultana, R. (2009). Competence and competence frameworks in career guidance: complex and contested concepts. *International Journal of Educational and Vocational Guidance,* (9), pp.15–30.

Useful resources

Below are some materials that you might find useful and interesting when exploring competence frameworks.

Canadian Standards and Guidelines for Career Development Practitioners: http://career-dev-guidelines.org/career_dev

Career Development Progression Pathway: www.thecdi.net/Career-Development-Sector-Progression-Pathway

Career Development Institute. (2015). Getting Qualified: www.thecdi.net/GettingQualified

Career Development Institute. (2015). Qualification in Career Guidance/Development: www.thecdi.net/Qualification-in-Career-Guidance

Scottish Benchmark Standards for a Master's level qualification in Career Guidance and Development: www.thecdi.net/Qualification-in-Career-Guidance

Career Industry Council of Australia Professional Standards: https://cica.org.au/professional-standards

International Association for Educational and Vocational Guidance (IAEVG): http://iaevg.net

National Career Development Association (NCDA, USA): www.ncda.org/aws/NCDA/pt/sp/guidelines

National Guidance Forum. (2007). *A Competency Framework for Guidance Practitioners*: www.nationalguidanceforum.ie/documents/NGF_Competency_Report Final.pdf

Network for Innovation in Career Guidance & Counselling in Europe (NICE): www.nice-network.eu

NOS Database: www.ukstandards.co.uk/Pages/index.aspx

Reflection page

9 | A–Z of CPD and developing your own career

Introduction

Undertaking CPD is not just about going on a course. The purpose of this chapter is to show you a range of different activities that you can do as part of your own continuous professional development. Depending on the way in which you learn best, some of these will suit you better than others. However, being open to trying new ways of learning is an important skill to develop and we hope that you will try many of the CPD methods suggested below.

A	ACTION RESEARCH
What this is: Action research is a process of self-reflection undertaken by practitioners within a social setting, their work-base for example. Its aim is to improve and develop practice. It is usually iterative, whereby change is continually reviewed as part of an ongoing process. It is a research method that is particularly useful for practitioners wanting to contribute to producing evidence-based practice.	
How this can be used as CPD: To explore areas of practice that you want to learn more about.	
Useful examples/websites: www.jeanmcniff.com/ar-booklet.asp www.aral.com.au/resources/guide.html	
Further information in this book: Chapter 5	

A	ASSESSMENT
What this is: Observing practice or written work against a set of previously agreed criteria to determine if the criteria have been met and providing constructive feedback.	
How this can be used as CPD: Having your own practice or written work assessed against set criteria can be a very useful way of determining which areas of your own practice are strong and which may require further development. Assessing someone else's	

work or practice can be beneficial too, as you may notice things which you would like to incorporate into your own practice. It can also help you to hone your own skills on providing constructive feedback.
Useful examples/websites: You could use the performance criteria in the National Occupational Standards: Career Development (NOS: CD) or performance criteria from vocational qualifications, such as the Level 6 Diploma in Career Guidance and Development. www.thecdi.net/National-Occupational-Standards www.ocr.org.uk/qualifications/vocational-qualifications-qcf-career-guidance-and-development-level-6-diploma-10215/
Further information in this book: Chapter 8

A	ASSOCIATION OF GRADUATE CAREERS ADVISORY SERVICES
What this is: 'The Association of Graduate Careers Advisory Services (AGCAS) is the professional body for careers and employability professionals working with higher education students and graduates and prospective entrants to higher education.' (From www.agcas.org.uk.) As stated on its website, its aims are to provide a lobbying voice for its membership; be the focal point for sector-wide research and expert opinion; provide a range of support and development opportunities for its members; promote standards for excellence in service delivery; conduct, gather and disseminate research intelligence on higher education and the graduate labour market; deliver high-quality training, development opportunities and events; and offer peer support, mentoring and networking.	
How this can be used as CPD: Having looked at what your CPD needs are, have a look at the websites below and see what is on offer.	
Useful examples/websites: www.agcas.org.uk www.agcasscotland.org.uk/fti	
Further information in this book: Chapter 3	

B	BLOGGING
What this is: Blogs (truncation of the expression 'weblog') are discussions and points of information on a particular subject which are available on the internet. Blogs can be the work of individuals, whilst others may have many authors and can be professionally edited. Some blogs have a section where visitors can leave comments and others allow communication with other visitors and the author/s of the blog.	

How this can be used as CPD: Blogs can be a useful way of keeping up to date with developments in the sector and finding out what particular people think about a given topic. Being able to communicate with the blogger can also help to develop your own thinking. Starting your own blog can be a useful way of ordering your own thinking and expressing your views. It is also a very good way to publicise yourself and what you do.
Useful examples/websites: https://adventuresincareerdevelopment.wordpress.com/ www.cegnet.co.uk/blog http://creativecareercoaching.org/blog/
Further information in this book: Chapter 7

B	BUDDYING
What this is: A way to enable peers to support each other by sharing experiences, offering advice and providing a sounding board for ideas and problems. Buddying is different from mentoring, which is a more formal and structured relationship where the mentor is typically in a more senior role than the mentee. The strength of buddying is that it takes the view that both partners can offer support and opportunities to learn whatever role they fulfil.	
How this can be used as CPD: Acting as a buddy provides a good developmental opportunity to improve your communication skills and share your knowledge and experience. Having a buddy provides you with someone with whom you can share ideas and knowledge, talk through issues and develop solutions. They can also introduce you to other people in their network and vice versa.	
Useful examples/websites: www.ncvo-vol.org.uk/uploadedFiles/NCVO/What_we_do/Campaigning_Effectiveness/NEW_Projects/Would_Like_to_Meet_FAQs.pdf	
Further information in this book: Chapter 6	

C	CAREER DEVELOPMENT INSTITUTE (CDI)
What this is: The CDI is the professional body for the career development sector in the UK. Its website provides information on a wide range of training events, conferences, accredited training, Communities of Interest and webinars. CDI members can access a CPD Resources Area where they can find information on online learning, publications and live events all categorised under the	

17 National Occupational Standards: Career Development. Members and registrants can use a bespoke area of the website to plan, record, reflect and report upon their CPD. As a means of demonstrating that they are professionally qualified, abide by the Code of Ethics and undertake a minimum of 25 hours' CPD annually, members can join the UK Register of Career Development Professionals. Members also receive a fortnightly email with details of developments in the sector, a quarterly journal – *Career Matters* – and the bi-annual *NICEC Journal*.
How this can be used as CPD: You can determine your own CPD needs and then look at the CDI site to see how your needs can be met. Reading CDI News via Email, *Career Matters* and the *NICEC Journal* will keep you up to date with sector developments and provide sources of information to help you to develop your professional knowledge and skills.
Useful examples/websites: www.thecdi.net
Further information in this book: Chapter 3

C	CASE STUDIES (REFLECTIVE)
What this is: A written reflection on an aspect of your work.	
How this can be used as CPD: Writing a case study can be a useful means of reflecting on a particular incident: describing what happened, why it happened, what you did, what informed this decision, what the outcome was (positive or negative) and whether or not you would act in the same way in the future. Reading case studies produced by other people can also be a useful source of information on how to deal with particular situations. You can also share your case studies as a means of disseminating effective practice in a particular area of your work.	
Further information in this book: Chapter 8	

C	COMMUNITIES OF INTEREST
What this is: A Community of Interest (COI) is a gathering of people assembled around a topic of common interest. Its members take part in the community to exchange information, to obtain answers to questions or problems, to improve their understanding of a subject or to share common issues. These can take place either face-to-face or online.	

How this can be used as CPD: These are a great way to find out what is happening in a particular part of the sector, to ask and answer questions, find out what others think, network and seek solutions to issues. You can join an existing COI or set up one of your own. Sometimes a COI will work together on a particular project and develop new materials that everyone can share.
Useful examples/websites: www.thecdi.net/Communities-of-Interest www.cegnet.co.uk
Further information in this book: Chapters 6 and 7

C	CONFERENCES, UK and INTERNATIONAL
What this is: These are usually events of one or more days' duration at which a range of keynote speeches are delivered and workshops offered on specific topics.	
How this can be used as CPD: Attending a conference provides you with the opportunity to hear the latest thinking on given subjects, attend workshops and network with others from your sector. This is a great way to undertake a lot of CPD in a short space of time. It is, however, important to reflect on what you learn and think through how you will use this in your practice. It can be too easy to return to work and not put your new learning into practice. Organising conferences can be a useful way of developing planning and networking skills, as well as having the opportunity to influence what will be offered by the speakers and workshops. Delivering papers or workshops provides you with the opportunity to research the topic you will be covering and to synthesise your thoughts into a paper or a workshop plan. Feedback from your presentation or workshop and networking with delegates can also increase your own knowledge of your particular topic.	
Useful examples/websites: www.thecdi.net/Skills-Training-Events www.agcas.org.uk/events?category=agcas_e	
Further information in this book: Chapters 6 and 7	

D	DAILY WORK
What this is: Anything that you do as part of your work role.	
How this can be used as CPD: In some respects every day can be seen as a training day. Being alert to naturally occurring opportunities to develop your learning is a skill worth developing.	

For example, a casual conversation with a colleague in which they share some useful information; or a chat over lunch about an article you have read, what you learned and how you are now using this information, which then leads to further conversation on other ways of using this information, can be seen as CPD. If you also develop the habit of writing this down in a CPD record then the act of actually recording it can help to reinforce the learning.
Further information in this book: Chapter 2

E	ETHICAL CASE STUDIES
What this is: These have been produced by members of the CDI Professional Standards Committee (PSC) and use a framework to approach a series of ethical issues based on the 12 principles in the CDI Code of Ethics.	
How this can be used as CPD: You could read one of the case study scenarios, think through how you would approach this situation and then read what the PSC members suggest. Alternatively, you could write an ethical case study of your own and use the framework to structure your response.	
Useful examples/websites: www.thecdi.net/Code-of-Ethics---Case-Studies	
Further information in this book: Chapter 4	

E	EVALUATION
What this is: Evaluation is a process that helps to assess whether something has worked and if it has achieved its aims and objectives. It is often used in research to assess if projects have achieved what they set out to do, and, if not, why not. It is a process that focuses on identifying learning from systematically reviewing an activity.	
How this can be used as CPD: You may want to evaluate how a training course you have attended has helped to develop your practice. Assess what the course was meant to deliver and if this has actually happened for you.	
Useful examples/websites www.heacademy.ac.uk/resources/resource2322 www.proveandimprove.org/documents/LBE.PDF	
Further information in this book: Chapter 5	

E	EXPERIENTIAL LEARNING
What this is: Experiential learning is the process through which an individual learns through the act of doing. It is closely linked to reflection and facilitates the development of practice through real life activities. David Kolb has written extensively about this.	
How this can be used as CPD: All new activities can provide an example to learn. For example, you may learn about applying for jobs online by completing an online application form.	
Useful examples/websites: http://infed.org/mobi/david-a-kolb-on-experiential-learning/ www.businessballs.com/kolblearningstyles.htm	
Further information in this book: Chapter 4	

F	FORMAL QUALIFICATIONS
What this is: These are qualifications that are accredited and awarded by a university or awarding organisation.	
How this can be used as CPD: Having determined your CPD needs, you may decide to undertake an accredited qualification. You may wish to do a full qualification or, if available, units or modules from one that meets your particular needs.	
Useful examples/websites: www.thecdi.net/Post-Graduate-Level-CPD www.thecdi.net/Certificate-in-Careers-Leadership www.thecdi.net/QCF-Qualifications-	
Further information in this book: Chapter 10	

G	GOOGLE BOOKS
What this is: Google Books is a service from Google Inc. that searches the full text of books and magazines that Google has scanned, converted to text using optical character recognition, and stored in its digital database. Books are provided either by publishers and authors, through the Google Books Partner Program, or by Google's library partners, through the Library Project. Additionally, Google has partnered with a number of magazine publishers to digitise their archives.	
How this can be used as CPD: Simply putting career development into the search facility will bring up a whole list of books on this subject, or you may prefer to search by title. Reading a book or chapter can be a useful source of knowledge and you can reflect on what you have learned and how you can use this in your practice.	
Useful examples/websites: https://books.google.com/?hl=en	

G	GOOGLE+
What this is: An interest-based social network.	
How this can be used as CPD: This can be used as a means to teach, share and learn through Google+ hangouts. There is a free online video-conferencing tool as a webinar platform or learning/teaching tool. This can be a useful source of CPD for you, but Google+ can also help you to create an online presence; engage with more people; find Communities of Interest and people with common interests; save money, as it is free to use; have real conversations; benefit from an array of tools; use your creativity to build a substantial profile and stand out when you engage with potential employers/clients.	
Useful examples/websites: https://plus.google.com/	
Further information in this book: Chapters 6 and 7	

G	GOOGLE SCHOLAR
What this is: Google Scholar is a freely accessible web search engine that indexes the full text or metadata of scholarly literature across an array of publishing formats and disciplines.	
How this can be used as CPD: You can use this to search for academic literature on a variety of topics. Abstracts are provided that describe the main content of the publication. Sometimes this will be for a publication that can be downloaded for a fee. At other times you may find a free-to-use pdf version of the publication that you need. Simply putting career development into the search function will give you an idea of the wealth of academic literature available. Reading a book or an article can be a useful source of knowledge, and you can reflect on what you have learned and how you can use this in your practice.	
Useful examples/websites: https://scholar.google.co.uk/	
Further information in this book: Chapter 5	

H	HELPING COLLEAGUES
What this is: Providing help to a colleague; for example, someone new to using the new computer system at work.	
How this can be used as CPD: This can help you to think through what you yourself know about the system in order to explain it to someone else. It can hone your training skills and, depending on how easily your colleague understands what you have said, it can enable you to reflect on the ways in which you explain new things to people.	
Further information in this book: Chapters 7 and 8	

I	IN-SERVICE TRAINING
What this is: This is training that is provided by your employer. It may be training that you have requested as part of your professional development or it may be training that everyone has to undertake – for example, on new legislation.	
How this can be used as CPD: This can be used to meet your identified CPD needs and should be planned, recorded, reflected upon and then put into practice. It is also a useful way of networking with colleagues; remember that a casual work-related conversation over lunch can often increase your knowledge.	
Further information in this book: Chapter 2	

I	INTERNATIONAL CENTRE FOR GUIDANCE STUDIES (iCeGS)
What this is: iCeGS is an international research centre with expertise in employability and career development. The centre conducts research, provides consultancy, offers a range of training and delivers a number of accredited learning programmes up to and including doctoral level. Staff are involved in undertaking research across the world; advising governments, careers and employability providers, educational organisations; and working with practitioners.	
How this can be used as CPD: The centre has a free regular newsletter, a mailing list and an annual lecture.	
Useful examples/websites: www.derby.ac.uk/icegs	
Further information in this book: Chapter 3	

J	JOURNALS
What this is: Journals are publications (either paper-based or electronic) written by experts in the sector as a means of disseminating their knowledge or research. Some are academic in focus and others less so but still a source of information and knowledge.	
How this can be used as CPD: Reading relevant articles, reflecting on what you have learned and thinking through how you will put this into practice, doing this and then reflecting again is a valuable CPD activity. Sharing what you have read at a meeting or including it in a blog is a further way of synthesising and embedding what you have learned.	

Useful examples:
British Journal of Guidance and Counselling *Career Matters* *NICEC Journal* *International Journal for Educational and Vocational Guidance*
Further information in this book: Chapter 6

K	KNOWLEDGE SHARING
What this is: Taking the time to share knowledge with colleagues.	
How this can be used as CPD: For example, having read an article, watched a webinar, attended a conference, etc. you will be in possession of some new knowledge which you could share with colleagues at a meeting, via a blog, a Community of Interest, network meeting, etc. Doing this will help to embed what you have learned but may also result in colleagues sharing new knowledge with you. Further discussion will lead to a greater understanding of what you know.	
Further information in this book: Chapter 6	

L	LECTURES
What this is: An educational talk to an audience.	
How this can be used as CPD: Having determined your CPD needs, you may like to look for any lectures that are being held that meet any of your needs. Attending lectures helps to develop your enquiring spirit. Lectures are often recorded and can be accessed online after the event. Alternatively, going to a lecture on a career development subject can often provide food for further thought and reflection and lead to wanting to learn more about that particular topic.	
Useful examples/websites: iCeGS annual lectures Inaugural lectures NICEC www.derby.ac.uk/education/institute-of-education/news/tristram-hooley-inaugural-lecture/	
Further information in this book: Chapter 7	

L	LINKEDIN
What this is: LinkedIn is a business-oriented social networking service. It is mainly used for professional networking.	
How this can be used as CPD: LinkedIn can be used to raise your professional profile and to develop your own network. Networking is not just about networking for today but also for the future. It is also a great source of knowledge on career paths, employers, jobs and industries.	
Useful examples/websites: www.linkedin.com	
Further information in this book: Chapters 6 and 7	

L	LUNCHING AND LEARNING
What this is: A form of networking where people come together for lunch or coffee to share their knowledge.	
How this can be used as CPD: Having a regular time each month where a group of professionals meet together to discuss a particular topic that one of the group has researched and leads upon can provide a valuable new source of learning in an informal atmosphere. The act of undertaking the research and leading the session is useful as CPD, as is hearing the information and the discussion that follows.	
Further information in this book: Chapter 6	

M	MENTORING
What this is: A relationship in which a more experienced or more knowledgeable person helps to guide a less experienced or less knowledgeable person who wants to learn.	
How this can be used as CPD: Having a mentor can provide a means of professional support. Someone with whom to sound out your ideas and from whom you can also learn. Your mentor can provide you with advice and encouragement; help you to solve problems for yourself; encourage you to reflect on your practice; and help you to improve your self-confidence. Being a mentor yourself can also be a great source of CPD, and you may find that many of the interpersonal skills you already have as a career development practitioner will equip you well for this role. Being a mentor can give you the opportunity to reflect on your own practice; enhance your role satisfaction; help you to develop professional relationships; enhance recognition from your peers;	

provide the satisfaction of making your experience available to another person; widen your knowledge of the sector and the way it works; and enhance your self-confidence in your professional skills and knowledge. You may also learn new ideas and methods from your mentee and make new contacts that will enhance your own professional network.
Further information in this book: Chapter 6

M	MOOCs
What this is: A MOOC (Massive Open Online Course) is an online course aimed at unlimited participation and open access via the web. In addition to traditional course materials, such as filmed lectures, readings and problem sets, many MOOCs provide interactive user forums to support further discussion among participants.	
How this can be used as CPD: Determining your CPD needs and then finding a relevant MOOC, or just seeing what MOOCs are available, and participating to see what you can learn and use in your professional practice.	
Useful examples/websites: www.mooc-list.com	
Further information in this book: Chapter 7	

N	NATIONAL GUIDANCE RESEARCH FORUM
What this is: The National Guidance Research Forum (NGRF) facilitates knowledge sharing and professional development, together with labour market information (LMI) for those interested in career guidance research and practice.	
How this can be used as CPD: Look at the website and explore what is on offer, e.g. LMI Online Learning Modules can help you to understand how to use LMI in your role.	
Useful examples/websites: www2.warwick.ac.uk/fac/soc/ier/ngrf	
Further information in this book: Chapters 3 and 5	

N	NATIONAL INSTITUTE FOR CAREER EDUCATION AND COUNSELLING (NICEC)
What this is: NICEC is a fellowship of people committed to understanding and developing career education and guidance practice and policy in the UK and across the globe. Their website aims to inform visitors of latest developments, NICEC events and	

news related to the *NICEC Journal*. Fellows and NICEC members have access to the journal and event materials via the members' site. Twice a year a joint NICEC/CDI conference is held which is free to attend, and CDI members receive the *NICEC Journal* twice a year free of charge.
How this can be used as CPD: Attending the conferences and seminars can really help to stimulate your thinking, as these are based on the latest research and how this can be used in practice. Articles in the *NICEC Journal* are also based on the latest research and thinking and are a very useful source of information. Attending events or reading articles and reflecting on how these can influence your practice is a good source of CPD.
Useful examples/websites: www.nicecjournal.org
Further information in this book: Chapter 8

N	NATIONAL OCCUPATONAL STANDARDS
What this is: National Occupational Standards (NOS) are statements of the skills, knowledge and understanding needed for effective performance in a job role and represent a consensus view and description of best practice for each particular function, having been developed and agreed with a range of employers and stakeholders representing the sector area. They can be regarded as the benchmark of competence required in the sector and form the key component of many qualifications.	
How this can be used as CPD: You can use the NOS: CD or others to provide a means of determining gaps in knowledge, experience and skills; NOS offer an objective process for determining your training needs and support your professional development.	
Useful examples/websites: www.thecdi.net/National-Occupational-Standards	
Further information in this book: Chapter 8	

N	NETWORKING
What this is: Using a supportive system of sharing information and services among individuals and groups having a common interest; this can be either in person or virtual.	
How this can be used as CPD: You can ask questions; share/learn new knowledge; promote your own business/expertise; develop your personal skills, including the use of technology to network; make connections that will be useful for your clients or	

your own business; and trade CPD opportunities. Setting up your own network can also help with all of the above as well as helping to develop organisational and communication skills.
Useful examples/websites: www.linkedin.com https://plus.google.com/ www.thecdi.net/Communities-of-Interest
Further information in this book: Chapter 6

N	NEWSLETTERS
What this is: Provide information of interest to members, customers, or employees. Many newsletters are now delivered electronically.	
How this can be used as CPD: These can be an excellent way to keep up to date about developments in the sector, forthcoming training events, research, employer news, vacancies, new resources and suggestions on how to get involved in the sector. The fact that an email newsletter drops into your inbox saves you time, as this information is instantly accessible. Electronic newsletters often have links for further information if you want to know more about a particular topic.	
Useful examples/websites: CDI News via Email (members only) iCeGS: www.derby.ac.uk/icegs Education and Employers: www.educationandemployers.org Pearson UK Policy Watch: http://uk.pearson.com/home/policy-watch.html Mindtools: www.mindtools.com The *Guardian* online has a number of newsletters on career topics.	
Further information in this book: Chapters 3 and 7	

O	OBSERVATIONS OF PRACTICE
What this is: Observing another practitioner undertaking a particular activity.	
How this can be used as CPD: Simply watching how someone else does their job can be a useful way to look at your own practice. What do they do that you could incorporate in your role? Is there anything they do that you would do differently? Being able to discuss what has taken place is also a useful way of developing our own skills and knowledge. Being observed yourself and then having such a discussion can also help you to reflect on your own practice and	

how this can be developed. NB: *This is different to assessment, where specific criteria are used in the observation of the practice and judgements made regarding competence.*
Useful examples: Reid, H. (2007) 'Structuring support and supervision for different contexts'. In: Harrison, R., Benjamin, C., Curran, S. and Hunter, R., eds. *Leading Work with Young People.* London: Sage Publications Ltd. pp. 164–76. ISBN 9781412946049.
Further information in this book: Chapter 4

O	ONLINE LEARNING
What this is: Learning which you do via the internet. There is a huge variety of different programmes available.	
How this can be used as CPD: Having determined your CPD needs, you can see what online learning may be available to meet them. You need to consider how you learn best, how you will evidence your learning and how you can put this into practice and reflect on what you have learned.	
Useful examples/websites: See above re MOOCs and below re OpenLearn. The CDI CPD Resources section for CDI members has information on various online learning opportunities and a guide to online learning.	
Further information in this book: Chapter 7	

O	OPENLEARN
What this is: Free online learning from The Open University. OpenLearn gives you free access to course materials and expert opinion on topical issues.	
How this can be used as CPD: Having determined your CPD needs, you can look at this site and search to see what is available that may help you.	
Useful examples/websites: www.open.edu/openlearn	
Further information in this book: Chapter 7	

P	PEER REVIEW
What this is: Peer review is the evaluation of work by one or more people of similar competence to the producers of the work. Peer review methods are employed to maintain standards of quality, improve performance and provide credibility. In the academic world,	

scholarly peer review is often used to determine an academic paper's suitability for publication.
How this can be used as CPD: Having peers provide feedback on your work can help you to see where its strengths lie and where there is a need for further development. Being the person who provides the feedback can help you to learn from others' work and, in turn, inform your own development.
Further information in this book: Chapter 5

P	PEST ANALYSIS
What this is: PEST analysis is a tool that helps you analyse the Political, Economic, Social and Technological changes in your environment. This helps you understand the 'big picture' forces of change that you are exposed to, and, from this, take advantage of the opportunities that they present. You can also add to this Legal and Environment changes: PESTLE.	
How this can be used as CPD: Doing this can help you to see what PEST changes you need to update yourself on, add this to your CPD plan and determine what you need to do in order to take advantage of the changes. For example, changes in legislation and how this may affect your role; changes in government policy; use of a new form of technology, etc.	
Useful examples/websites: www.cipd.co.uk/hr-resources/factsheets/pestle-analysis.aspx	
Further information in this book: Chapter 6	

P	PODCASTS
What this is: A podcast is a downloadable audio file made available through the internet.	
How this can be used as CPD: Some organisations will record seminars and sessions and make them available on their websites. This is useful if you are not able to attend a seminar or lecture. There are also lots of university careers services that have downloadable podcasts focusing on occupational information topics. Some open learning materials will also use podcasts to share learning.	
Useful examples/websites: www.careers.cam.ac.uk/podcasts/podcastsIndex.asp www.careerjoy.com/podcasts www.theguardian.com/careers/podcasts-jobs-audio	
Further information in this book: Chapter 10	

P	PROFESSIONAL DISCUSSION
What this is: This is usually used as an assessment method in vocational qualifications, whereby the candidate has a structured conversation with their assessor as a means for the candidate to demonstrate the learning outcomes through exploration, discussion and probing of practice and underpinning knowledge and principles.	
How this can be used as CPD: For CPD purposes the same process can be used. You could ask a colleague to ask you what you know about certain knowledge/understanding criteria from the National Occupational Standards: Career Development. They could ask you questions and challenge your thinking. You could then reverse the process. Mutual learning and sharing of knowledge will be a benefit of this process, as well as determining any areas for further development.	
Further information in this book: Chapter 4	

P	PROFESSIONAL MEMBERSHIP
What this is: Being a member of a professional body can help you to acquire, develop and maintain your professional status and to promote the career development sector as a profession.	
How this can be used as CPD: Professional body membership usually allows you access to CPD resources, newsletters, journals, magazines, website information, a means of recording your CPD, networking opportunities, conferences, events, webinars, etc.	
Useful examples/websites: www.agcas.org.uk www.thecdi.net www.cipd.co.uk http://iaevg.net/	
Further information in this book: Chapter 3	

P	PROGRESSION PATHWAY
What this is: The CDI Career Development Sector Progression Pathway acknowledges the wide range of roles performed across the profession from first contact through to support roles, practitioner, specialist practitioner, manager, senior manager and specialist roles in lecturing, consultancy, inspecting and research and the ways in which a person can progress their career. It shows the interrelationship between the different branches of the profession: career education, career guidance/development and career coaching/talent management and the career mobility that is possible between them. Based on the National Occupational Standards: Career Development, it shows what skills and knowledge are needed for each role and the relevant qualifications.	

How this can be used as CPD: If you want to move from one level of role to another you can use this to see what is involved and what qualifications you will need. You can also see how your existing skills and knowledge relate to your preferred role and how you can use informal CPD as well as formal qualifications to develop these.
Useful examples/websites: www.thecdi.net/Career-Development-Sector-Progression-Pathway
Further information in this book: Chapter 3

P	PROJECT WORK
What this is: Undertaking a piece of work or activity with a particular aim in a specified period of time.	
How this can be used as CPD: Undertaking a project can help you to develop new skills and knowledge. It often involves researching what has been done before, planning the project, delivery, evaluation and dissemination of results. Building time in to the work in order to reflect on what you did and why, and if you would do the same thing again or differently can be a really useful source of CPD.	
Further information in this book: Chapter 5	

P	PUBLICATIONS
What this is: Any written material on a particular topic that has been published; this can be books, papers, reports, PhD theses, journals, magazines, newspapers, etc.	
How this can be used as CPD: Reading publications can be a useful means of updating your knowledge of the sector, of theories, new practices, etc. Writing a book or for a journal or magazine is a great source of CPD as it demands research skills as well as the ability to crystallise your thoughts so that they can be understood by your audience.	
Useful examples/websites: www.thecdi.net/Reports---Resources (open access) CDI CPD Resources Area (members only) has a range of publications listed under each of the 17 National Occupational Standards: Career Development. www.derby.ac.uk/research/icegs/publications www.agcas.org.uk/pages/publications	
Further information in this book: Chapter 3	

Q	QUALITY ASSURANCE
What this is: In developing products and services, quality assurance is the systematic process of checking to see whether a product or service being developed is meeting specified requirements.	
How this can be used as CPD: Undertaking a quality assurance process involves learning about what should be done and then comparing actual practice or process to this. This can help you to improve your own knowledge about a particular process or product as well as developing your skills of giving constructive feedback. Having your own practice or products quality assured is a useful means of finding out how this meets the quality criteria and what areas require development.	

Q	QUESTIONING COLLEAGUES
How this can be used as CPD: Colleagues are a very accessible source of knowledge and information. Do not limit yourself to just asking questions of those people with more experience than you. Asking more recently qualified colleagues their views can also be an excellent source of information, especially about new developments. Remember, too, that other colleagues in non-professional roles will also have interesting knowledge to share with you. Questioning of colleagues can also take place virtually via online networks and Communities of Interest.	
Useful examples/websites: www.linkedin.com https://plus.google.com/ www.thecdi.net/Communities-of-Interest	
Further information in this book: Chapter 5	

R	REFLECTION ON PRACTICE
What this is: This is the process through which we examine our practice and learn from what we observe. It is a critical activity whereby we use opportunities that we feel have worked well and those that worked less well to examine what contributed to the successful or less successful outcome. This activity is closely linked to experiential learning.	

How this can be used as CPD: This is a core activity for the professional career development practitioner. It can be used after an interview or a group work activity to assess what worked well, whether the participant(s) got what they needed from the interaction, and what you can do to improve for next time.
Useful examples/websites: Bassot, B. (2013). *The Reflective Journal.* London: Palgrave Macmillan. Findley, L. (2008). *Reflecting on Reflective Practice.* Milton Keynes: The Open University. Paper 52 Practice Based Professional Learning Centre. Available at: www.open.ac.uk/opencetl/sites/www.open.ac.uk.opencetl/files/files/ecms/web-content/Finlay-(2008)-Reflecting-on-reflective-practice-PBPL-paper-52.pdf. Smith, M. (1999). Reflection, learning and education. Infed. Available at: http://infed.org/mobi/reflection-learning-and-education.
Further information in this book: Chapter 4

R	RESEARCH
What this is: There are many different definitions used to describe research, but it is basically a systematic approach used for solving a problem or creating new knowledge. It consists of a set of techniques that can be applied within different contexts to investigate/explore/examine an area of interest.	
How this can be used as CPD: Research can be used in many ways. You can read research reports to find out what is new in the careers world; you can undertake your own research project to investigate any problem or an idea you might have; and you can contribute to research projects and share your views.	
Useful examples/websites: CDI News via Email (members only) NICEC: www.nicecjournal.org iCeGS: www.derby.ac.uk/icegs NGRF: www2.warwick.ac.uk/fac/soc/ier/ngrf Institute for Employment Studies: www.employment-studies.co.uk Warwick Institute for Employment Research: www2.warwick.ac.uk/fac/soc/ier/research Centre for Career and Personal Development: www.canterbury.ac.uk/education/our-work/centre-for-career-and-personal-development/our-research.aspx	
Further information in this book: Chapter 5	

S	SECONDMENT
What this is: Secondment is the temporary transfer of a practitioner to another position or department.	
How this can be used as CPD: A secondment can give you the opportunity for wider career and personal development than in your day-to-day work. It can help you to acquire valuable experience in project management and provide the opportunity to test and apply specific skills in a different organisational environment. You can also gain new skills and experiences in more challenging areas. It can improve your team skills and add valuable contacts to your professional network.	
Useful examples/websites: www.cipd.co.uk/hr-resources/factsheets/secondment.aspx	

S	SEMINARS
What this is: Seminars are a form of instruction, bringing together small groups for recurring meetings, focusing each time on a particular subject, in which everyone present is requested to actively participate.	
How this can be used as CPD: Attending a seminar can enhance your knowledge of a particular subject, both from the seminar leader and your fellow participants. Leading a seminar can do this too, as you will need to research your topic and will learn from the views of the participants.	
Useful examples/websites: NICEC: www.nicecjournal.org/events	
Further information in this book: Chapter 7	

S	SOCIAL MEDIA
What this is: These are computer-mediated tools facilitating opportunities to create, share and exchange information and resources.	
How this can be used as CPD: Social media is a really useful way to extend your network through participating in discussion forums.	
Useful examples/websites: www.linkedin.com www.facebook.com www.twitter.com	
Further information in this book: Chapter 7	

S	SUPERVISION
What this is: Supervision is a positive and enabling process that brings a practitioner and a skilled supervisor together to reflect on work practice. It is the process by which a practitioner can review and evaluate their work through discussion, reporting and observation with another worker. Supervision aims to identify solutions to problems, improve practice and increase understanding of professional issues.	
How this can be used as CPD: Supervision helps you to develop knowledge and skills and to reflect on your practice and its adherence to a relevant code of ethics. It helps to ensure that professional standards are maintained and that policies and procedures of the organisation are adhered to. It is underpinned by learning from experience and reflective practice. Engaging with an experienced worker who is prepared to help you look critically at what you do can help you to gain a better understanding, in professional terms, of your work situation. It helps you to keep your practice fresh and to manage the pressures of your role.	
Further information in this book: Chapter 4	

T	TEACHING
What this is: This can be formal and informal, and involves the imparting of skills and/or knowledge to others.	
How this can be used as CPD: Preparing for a teaching session, including thinking through how you will meet the learning needs of your audience, is a useful source of CPD as it enables you to research your subject matter and synthesise and interpret this so that others may benefit. The actual act of teaching and discussion with the learners can also add their perspectives to your own knowledge.	

T	TED TALKS
What this is: This is a large bank of inspiring and sometimes offbeat talks, typically of about 20 minutes' duration, which can be searched by topic.	
How this can be used as CPD: Having analysed your CPD needs, you can search the TED website to see if there are any TED Talks that meet your needs. Alternatively, looking through what is there can help improve your spirit of enquiry and curiosity, and you never know what you might find that helps you with your professional practice.	

Useful examples/websites: www.ted.com/talks Body language example: www.ted.com/talks?q=amy+cuddy&sort=newest
Further information in this book: Chapter 7

T	TRAINING SESSION
What this is: An event run on a particular topic. These may be made compulsory by an employer and cover such topics as legislation or new company working practices, or they may be sessions that you choose to do having analysed your own CPD needs. Training events can be non-accredited or may be part of a formal programme of learning, leading to a qualification.	
How this can be used as CPD: These can be a valuable source of learning and help to develop skills and knowledge. You can also use them as an opportunity to network; it is worth thinking through beforehand who will be attending the event and some questions that you would like to ask of the people you meet.	
Useful examples/websites: www.thecdi.net/Developing-Yourself www.agcas.org.uk/events?category=agcas_e http://shop.cipd.co.uk/shop/cipd-training/	
Further information in this book: Chapter 2	

T	TWITTER
What this is: Twitter is an online social networking service that enables users to send and read short 140-character messages called 'tweets'.	
How this can be used as CPD: Twitter can be used as a means of keeping yourself up to date with sector developments by following key people or organisations. It can also alert you to training opportunities and other CPD events.	
Useful examples/websites: https://twitter.com/?lang=en-gb @theCDI	
Further information in this book: Chapter 7	

U	UPDATING COLLEAGUES
What this is: Passing on knowledge to colleagues that you have learned from attending an event or from your own reading or research.	
How this can be used as CPD: Having attended an event or undertaken some reading/research you will be able to think through what you have learned and which aspects of this will be of benefit to your colleagues. Reflecting in this way on what you have learned helps you to embed what you have learned, and the act of updating colleagues allows you to articulate this, which further embeds your knowledge as well as providing you with the opportunity to hear the perspectives of others on what you have learned.	
Further information in this book: Chapter 7	

U	USER GROUPS
What this is: A group of people focused on the use of a particular product. This can be around using new types of technology, but could be broader than this and cover the use of a particular product or service.	
How this can be used as CPD: Being involved in the testing or evaluation of a new product is a useful way to find out about the product and to think through how you could use this in your own practice. It also hones your own skills of evaluation, reporting and providing constructive feedback, as well as the opportunity to hear the views of others in the group.	

V	VIMEO
What this is: A video-sharing website on which users can upload, share and view videos. It is also used by universities and others for recording lectures.	
How this can be used as CPD: Having looked at your CPD needs, you can search Vimeo to see if there are any videos there that would help to meet your needs.	
Useful examples/websites: https://vimeo.com/join	

V	VISITING OTHER PROVIDERS
What this is: Using opportunities to network with colleagues, visit their services or centres and build up your referral contacts.	

How this can be used as CPD: Being able to see how a different organisation provides their services can inspire your own thinking. Thinking through the questions you want to ask before the visit can help you to clarify your own thoughts about the way you deliver your services and you can then compare and contrast this with the services offered elsewhere. This is also a useful source of networking.
Further information in this book: Chapter 7

V	VOCATIONAL QUALIFICATIONS
What this is: Vocational qualifications offer practical learning programmes that relate to specific job roles or employment sectors. They are designed to help learning in a practical way about a specific job area.	
How this can be used as CPD: Undertaking a vocational qualification can help you to learn specific skills and knowledge for your current or future work role. It is often possible to take units from a vocational qualification, rather than the whole qualification, if you want to develop a specific area of your practice.	
Useful examples/websites: www.ocr.org.uk http://qualifications.pearson.com/en/home.html www.cityandguilds.com	
Further information in this book: Chapter 2	

V	VOCOPHER
What this is: The purpose of Vocopher is to provide researchers and counsellors with resources with which to further their research and assist their clients respectively. These services are provided free of charge in the hope that others will join in this collaborative effort. The site contains career construction materials and old (1990s) recordings of famous career theorists, including Donald Super and John Krumboltz.	
How this can be used as CPD: Having determined your CPD needs, you can search the Vocopher website for items of relevance to you. It is also worth having a general exploration of what is there and reading some of the documents/viewing some of the videos to see how these can inspire your creativity and thinking about your practice.	
Useful examples/websites: http://vocopher.com/	
Further information in this book: Chapter 7	

W	WEBINARS
What this is: Short for web-based seminar, a webinar is a presentation, lecture, workshop or seminar that is transmitted over the web using video-conferencing software. A key feature of a webinar is its interactive elements: the ability to give, receive and discuss information in real-time. Recordings of the webinar can sometimes be available for both participants and those who were unable to attend. These are different to webcasts in which the data transmission is one way and does not allow interaction between the presenter and the audience.	
How this can be used as CPD: Webinars can be used to meet your identified CPD needs or as a means of exploring new topics. As they can be offered and accessed from anywhere in the world, the range of webinars available is large.	
Useful examples/websites: www.thecdi.net/Skills-Training-Events	
Further information in this book: Chapter 7	

W	WORK-SHADOWING
What this is: This involves working with another employee who might do a different job, or have something to teach, or can help the person shadowing him or her to learn new aspects related to the job, organisation, certain behaviours, skills or knowledge.	
How this can be used as CPD: Having looked at your own CPD needs, you may decide that there is a colleague who can help you to meet these needs by allowing you to work-shadow them. If you are interested in a different role within your organisation, then work-shadowing someone in this role is a useful way of finding out about what is involved.	

W	WRITING
How this can be used as CPD: Writing enables you to clarify your own thoughts and present them in a way that others will understand. If what you write also involves you undertaking some research, then this further adds to your knowledge. You could write articles for journals and magazines, newsletters, academic papers, blogs or websites. Writing is also a good means of reflecting on your practice. The physical act of writing down what has happened during your working day will help you to reflect on what has happened and what you have learned as a result of this.	
Further information in this book: Chapter 4	

X	XYLOPHONE PLAYING – work/life balance and learning from your hobbies
What this is: It is important to strike a work/life balance and you have a duty of care to yourself to be fit and healthy to undertake your job role.	
How this can be used as CPD: Sometimes, hobbies or extra-curricular interests can be a useful source of CPD. You might run a local youth football team, and this can help you to develop knowledge about young people and hone your coaching skills. Local amateur dramatic groups are a useful way to develop self-confidence and speaking in public. Being on a committee helps to develop team-working skills. And so on. The important thing is to reflect on what your outside activities are and how these can be used to develop relevant skills and knowledge for your working life. Remember – every day is a training day, both inside and outside of work.	

Y	YOUTUBE
What this is: A video-sharing website.	
How this can be used as CPD: You can search YouTube for videos that may meet some of your identified CPD needs, or simply search on career development areas/topics and use your critical faculties to judge what is there and its relevance to your needs. Recordings of the CDI webinars are available via YouTube.	
Useful examples/websites: www.youtube.com/?hl=en-GB&gl=GB	
Further information in this book: Chapter 7	

Z	Zzzz
What this is: Sleep is restorative.	
How this can be used as CPD: Sometimes what can seem to be a problem can look much better after a good night's sleep. Sleep gives your brain the chance to recover and consolidate what you have learned, and your learning can benefit from this the following day, as will your powers of concentration and your ability to remember what you have learned.	

Reflection page

10 | Moving on – what you are going to do next!

Introduction

In this final chapter we want to provide some suggestions that will help you to make use of the activities in this book. In this section we will introduce you to:

- using CPD
- formal accreditation and qualifications
- supporting and developing your colleagues
- developing your CPD plan.

Using CPD

Throughout this book we have talked a lot about engaging in CPD activities. A major issue with CPD is that you can attend a workshop, read an article, listen to a podcast, and so on, but if you don't do anything with what you have done it is a waste of time and money. As trainers we find it disappointing when we have worked with people who seemed to have really engaged in activities and when we follow up with them to find out how they have got on we discover they have done nothing!

This may be for many reasons: not having the opportunity to use the new knowledge or skills, finding it too difficult or not having the outcomes they expected. The essential elements of CPD are using it and reflecting on it. So, when deciding what you are going to do for CPD, make sure you plan how you are going to use it. If you can't do this, then wait until you will have an opportunity to use it. A skill not used is a skill forgotten.

CPD is not just a series of interventions but it is a process whereby we assess our professional practice, identify areas for development and then explore how we might address the development needs. There is no one right way; it is about finding what is right for you. Throughout the book we have provided many suggestions. CPD should be an enjoyable experience; if you end up doing all the same things all the time it will be boring and you will lack motivation. We hope you will identify some new ways of developing your practice and let us know how you get on.

Formal accreditation and qualifications

One thing we have not focused a great deal on in this book is formal qualifications. There are lots of opportunities for you to seek formal accreditation for learning. For some people this is an important part of professional development as it provides recognition and certification of learning. Specifically, it offers transferability of learning between and across sectors. If you want to consider formal accreditation and qualifications it can be expensive, depending on what you want to do. If you are employed, it is worth having a chat with your boss about the organisational policy on this and test out if this is something they might be willing to invest in.

Although many people assume their employer will not contribute, many employers do offer some financial support: contributing towards course fees, or providing time off for study, or access to resources or clients. In our experience, if you do not ask you do not get! We have known a number of cases where people have had their master's degree paid for them by their employer. In one case, a student submitted her master's dissertation on the Thursday and retired on the Friday! This was an unusual case.

If you are going to ask your employer for support, you need to have your arguments ready as to why you believe doing the programme will contribute not just to your development but also to that of your organisation. Think about what the benefits might be to your colleagues, as well as any potential financial benefits to the organisation.

If you are looking at developing your qualifications, there are a number of options that you can pursue. This list is not definitive but just offers some suggestions.

Professional training for the careers sector

If you do not already have a professional qualification you might want to consider doing the **Level 6 Diploma in Career Guidance and Development**. This is a work-based learning qualification and is awarded by OCR and Pearson. You can choose to take the full Level 6 qualification or select units as part of your CPD for which you can seek accreditation. Information about this can be found at www.ocr.org.uk/qualifications/vocational-qualifications-qcf-career-guidance-and-development-level-6-diploma-10215/ and www.thecdi.net/QCF-Centres.

The **Qualification in Career Guidance/Development** (QCG/D) is the CDI-awarded higher education-based initial training award for the career development sector. This is available at a number of universities through either full-time, part-time or blended learning courses. The course is part of a postgraduate diploma or master's course. Information about courses can be found at www.thecdi.net/Qualification-in-Career-Guidance.

Practitioners working in schools may want to explore the above qualifications or focus on the **Certificate in Careers Leadership**: www.thecdi.net/Certificate-in-Careers-Leadership. In addition to this, there are a number of qualifications that focus on careers education courses available from QCG/D institutions.

Academic qualifications

If you would like to consider broader academic qualifications you might want to think about an undergraduate degree (BA, BSc), a master's (MA, MSc) or even a doctoral qualification (PhD, Ed.D). There are a small number of undergraduate degrees that focus on career guidance/counselling. For information about these or any other undergraduate awards look at www.ucas.com.

If you have already studied at undergraduate degree level or equivalent, you may want to consider doing a postgraduate or master's level qualification. There are a number that focus on career development and coaching practice. Information about these can be found at www.thecdi.net/Getting-Qualified/Masters-and-other-courses. Many of these courses are recognised by the CDI for registration with the UK Register of Career Development Professionals. You may of course want to do something not directly related to careers work, preferring a higher level qualification for your own interest. There are many options for modes of study: you can choose to study full time, part time, distance learning or e-learning. Many universities provide all these options; the Open University specialises in distance learning programmes for adult learners: www.open.ac.uk.

If you have an interest in research and would like to undertake in-depth research, you might want to consider either an MRes (Master of Research), MPhil (Master of Philosophy), a PhD (Doctor of Philosophy) or a professional doctorate such as a Doctor of Education (Ed.D); these qualifications may be known by different names in other countries. These can be taken full time (usually a minimum of three years) or part time (minimum of five to six years). Many doctoral routes include research methods training as part of the programme; an Ed.D, for example, is modular, and students will undertake modules focusing on developing their ideas and research skills before starting their research project. Information about doctoral study can be found at www.vitae.ac.uk/doing-research/doing-a-doctorate.

For many areas of practice there are specialist training and qualifications. If you are interested in developing your knowledge and skills in a particular area you might want to explore opportunities focusing on these. Some examples include:

- motivational interviewing
- cognitive behavioural therapy (CBT)
- psychometric testing
- counselling
- neuro-linguistic programming
- coaching
- mentoring.

There are a wide range of courses available for all of these; make sure you get recommendations from others before you commit as qualifications can be expensive.

Working with your colleagues

We find that many practitioners often undertake additional qualifications and training because they enjoy supporting their colleagues. Throughout this book we have focused CPD very much around you and how you develop yourself, although much of this is around building your networks and learning from others.

If you work for an employer, you might want to use some of the suggestions in this book to build a collegiate approach to CPD. We have seen some really excellent CPD where one member of staff learns something and then shares it with their colleagues. This is a really good way of reinforcing the learning as well as ensuring that more people benefit from the investment and engagement in the learning activities. In our organisations we do this as a matter of course in order to maximise the benefits from the investment. This is especially important when funding is tight and it is difficult to release people to engage in training.

Below are some recommendations as to ways in which you can maximise CPD through working with colleagues.

- Most organisations will undertake training needs analysis to identify where the skills gaps are – encourage your organisation to do a skills benefit analysis. Identify what the strengths are within the organisation and who has specialist skills that might be useful to other colleagues. This could be someone having a particular interest in career theory, reflective practice, ethics, social media or group work.

- Talk to your work colleagues and put together a list of the CPD that you all do by yourself, in order to utilise each other's knowledge and expertise. This is a great way of making CPD accessible, building confidence, sharing knowledge and standardising practice.
- Build in time at team meetings to update on intelligence or knowledge each of you might have learned since the last meeting.
- Build in time at team meetings to do short CPD inputs; different staff can take responsibility for organising and delivering the CPD activities.
- If there are skills gaps in the organisation, members of staff can be identified to go and acquire these skills and develop their knowledge.
- Encourage all staff to have an area of specialism. This might be around knowledge such as older workers, legislation, safeguarding; or it could focus on particular skills such as group work, using interest guides and motivating clients.

If you are self-employed you can still do all of the same activities with other self-employed peers. Regular training sessions could be delivered using Skype or through webinars. This also helps to keep down the costs of investment of time and money in training.

Developing your CPD plan

You are now at the end of the book, that is if you have read it all the way through, so congratulations! We hopefully have provided you with all the tools to help you understand why CPD is important and how you can invest in yourself to develop your professional practice. Appendix 2 contains a template that you can use to plan your CPD. This will help you to think about what you want to do, what you will do, what the benefits to you and others are, how you will measure the outcomes of your CPD and, finally, what the expected impact will be for your practice. This is just an example we use; feel free to use your own if you have one that works for you.

Below are a few suggestions that may help you start focusing on your CPD and what to do next.

- Select one of the competence frameworks in Chapter 8 and use it to identify the CPD that will help to enhance and grow your practice.

- Identify an approach that will work for you to reflect on your CPD; it may be something formal or less formal but think about how you can record and use this learning.
- Step outside of your comfort zone: move to being proactive in some of your CPD rather than always being a passive recipient.
- Review your online profile – if you don't have one, now is the time to set one up.
- Set yourself some targets as to how you will build your network and followers online.
- Plan your CPD so that you do something on a regular basis – you will need to evidence 25 hours annually if you are a CDI Registered Career Development Professional. Little and often is good.
- Select five new activities from the A–Z of CPD in Chapter 9 and try them out.
- Seek out opportunities for international CPD. This might be through an international LinkedIn group or find a conference and follow it using the hashtag # on Twitter.
- Think of a small research project you might like to do which will help to build the evidence base and enhance your practice.
- Find and read a research report on an area you are interested in.
- Submit an article to *Career Matters* on something you have done that you think other practitioners might be interested in.
- Start a blog!

Appendix 1 – Practitioner researcher project pro forma

Title of action research project:

Aims and objectives

What are the aims and objectives of the action research project? What do you hope to achieve?

Rationale

Why have you selected this project? Why is it important that this piece of work be done?

Literature to inform the study

What have you found out about studies/projects that have already been conducted?

Methods/design

Describe the approach you plan to take. Try and provide as much detail as you can.

Participants

Who will be included in your research? Clients/learners/colleagues.

Resources

What resources might you need, e.g. dictaphone, interview space, permission from managers.

Ethical considerations

What might the ethical considerations be, e.g. obtaining consent, confidentiality, etc.

Implementation

How have you implemented your research? What have you done?

Evaluation

How have you evaluated what you have done?

Publishing findings

What is your plan to share what you have learned?

Appendix 2 – CPD action plan

Area for development	Actions to be undertaken	Timescale	Benefit to self	Benefit to others	Measurement	Expected impact of actions
Build my online profile	1. Create a LinkedIn account. 2. Create a Twitter account.	By end of April	1. To extend my network and communicate with others. 2. To open up ways of gathering new information.	1. Will have new tools to communicate with clients and colleagues. 2. New methods for people to contact me.	1. Create a plan to promote myself online identifying targets. 2. To identify 30 people to follow. 3. To attract 30 followers. 4. To join six LinkedIn groups.	1. I will have developed my knowledge of social media tools and how to use them. 2. I will have a larger network 3. I will be able to contribute to discussions and share ideas with colleagues and peers. 4. I will have a profile online and people can contact me.

Index

Further reflection pages

Further reflection pages

Further reflection pages

Further reflection pages

Further reflection pages

Further reflection pages

Further reflection pages

Further reflection pages

Further reflection pages

Further reflection pages

Further reflection pages

Further reflection pages

Further reflection pages

Further reflection pages